Focus on the Future by my dear friend Tim Clinton is a must-read for the times we find ourselves in. Tim weaves together our storied past as followers of Christ, starting with the effect of the early Christians on the Roman Empire right through to today, as we navigate spiritual warfare on levels we have never experienced. There *is* a new attack on the family, but as Tim points out, there is still great hope for these troubled times, and *Focus on the Future* points the way forward.

—JENTEZEN FRANKLIN
SENIOR PASTOR, FREE CHAPEL
NEW YORK TIMES BEST-SELLING AUTHOR

I have been grateful to call Dr. Tim Clinton a friend for many years. He is a master in his field, bringing hope, healing, and godly perspective to the thousands of lives he impacts every day. This book, however, surprised me. Everything I expected to be there was there, but there was so much more. You will be deeply touched by Tim's vulnerability and tender heart. You will be drawn closer to Christ.

—SHEILA WALSH
AUTHOR, *PRAYING WOMEN* AND
PRAYING GIRLS DEVOTIONAL

Dr. Tim Clinton's dynamic new book, *Focus on the Future*, is a positive, hopeful message that is a pleasure to read and will motivate you to see good things in your family's future. While we see ugliness all about our national landscape, Dr. Clinton points to the beauty of timeless truths and gently reminds us these promises are yours and mine—to lean on. Thank you, Dr. Clinton, for writing this powerful book when Americans need this message most!

—HON. MICHELE BACHMANN
FORMER MEMBER, US HOUSE OF REPRESENTATIVES

Tim Clinton's new book, *Focus on the Future*, boldly forges the path for those who care about Christian values and culture. This is the book we've all been waiting for!

—Dr. Robert Jeffress
Senior Pastor, First Baptist Church, Dallas

With insights from history and Scripture, *Focus on the Future* helps us understand our current cultural moment, bringing clarity to our uncertain times and giving us a way forward. If we desire to protect our families and our freedoms, if we want to effect change in our nation here and now, then we need to be eternally minded people.

—Samuel Rodriguez
Senior Pastor, New Season Christian Worship Center
President, NHCLC; Author, *You Are Next!*
Executive Producer, *Breakthrough*

I have enjoyed watching Tim Clinton over the years as the Lord has prepared him to stand in the gap for our nation's future in this critical hour. In *Focus on the Future*, he masterfully outlines the foundation of Christianity in America. If you care about leaving a legacy of faith and freedom for your children and grandchildren, you need to read this book!

—Ralph Reed
Founder and Chairman, Faith and
Freedom Coalition

As we stand at the crossroads of faith and freedom, the importance of marriages and families as the bedrock of society has never been more crucial to our survival. Carrying the mantle of forerunners such as James Dobson, Tim Clinton delivers a Christian manifesto for the future that is both challenging and hopeful.

—Dr. Tony Evans
President, The Urban Alternative
Senior Pastor, Oak Cliff Bible Fellowship

Never before has our future seemed as dark and desperate. Yet into this crisis Tim Clinton courageously shines the bright light of biblical truth for all to see. A clarion call for Christians who recognize the signs of this critical time, *Focus on the Future* is one of those landmark books we will be referring to for years to come.

—PAULA WHITE-CAIN
OVERSEEING PASTOR, CITY OF DESTINY

How will our faith be tested in the days to come? Will we succumb to a culture that tramples truth underfoot? Or will we respond to the trumpet's call and fight for our families by upholding, defending, and living out those eternal values given to us by a loving God? Tim's book will teach you how to speak truth boldly, trust God more deeply, and create a legacy of faith triumphant. It's a must-read for the days in which we live.

—JANET PARSHALL
NATIONALLY SYNDICATED TALK SHOW HOST

As Dr. Tim Clinton writes, there is an urgency to contend for the faith and "pass a holy way of life on to generations yet unborn." The data is alarming. Loneliness and suicides are at all-time highs, fatherlessness abounds, and a staggering number of young people have no church involvement. Those of us who love the Lord must invest in the next generation. It will bear fruit because relationships heal and restore. Investing in the generations to come will transform individuals, families, communities, and churches—let's get engaged now, while it's not too late!

—JAMES ROBISON
FOUNDER AND PRESIDENT, LIFE OUTREACH INTERNATIONAL
FORT WORTH, TEXAS

A gift to the body of Christ, *Focus on the Future* isn't just what we need today. It is what we need to be ready for tomorrow. Throughout this book you will find clear, scriptural wisdom, which will inspire any reader to look ahead and answer the questions "How am I using my voice to defend the faith when faced with opposition?" and "How is my family protecting our values and forging ahead with the Great Commission amid a time of great confusion?" Thank you, Dr. Clinton, for another incredible resource.

—BECKY THOMPSON
BEST-SELLING AUTHOR, *LOVE UNENDING*
FOUNDER, MIDNIGHT MOM DEVOTIONAL PRAYER MOVEMENT

FOCUS
ON THE
FUTURE

DR. TIM CLINTON

Most Charisma Media products are available at special quantity discounts for bulk purchase for sales promotions, premiums, fundraising, and educational needs. For details, call us at (407) 333-0600 or visit our website at www.charismamedia.com.

FOCUS ON THE FUTURE by Tim Clinton
Published by FrontLine, an imprint of Charisma Media
600 Rinehart Road, Lake Mary, Florida 32746

Unless otherwise noted, all Scripture quotations are taken from the Holy Bible, New International Version®, NIV®. Copyright © 1973, 1978, 1984, 2011 by Biblica, Inc.® Used by permission of Zondervan. All rights reserved worldwide. www.zondervan.com. The "NIV" and "New International Version" are trademarks registered in the United States Patent and Trademark Office by Biblica, Inc.®

Scripture quotations marked ESV are from the Holy Bible, English Standard Version. Copyright © 2001 by Crossway Bibles, a division of Good News Publishers. Used by permission.

Scripture quotations marked KJV are from the King James Version of the Bible.

Scripture quotations marked NKJV are taken from the New King James Version®. Copyright © 1982 by Thomas Nelson. Used by permission. All rights reserved.

Visit the author's website at timclinton.com, timclintonbooks.com.

Cataloging-in-Publication Data is on file with the Library of Congress.

International Standard Book Number: 978-1-62999-734-6

E-book ISBN: 978-1-62999-735-3

21 22 23 24 25 — 987654321

Printed in the United States of America

*To my children, Megan and Zach, and their families.
"The LORD bless you and keep you; the LORD make His
face shine upon you, and be gracious to you; the LORD
lift up His countenance upon you, and give you peace"
(Num. 6:24–26, NKJV).*

The world can no longer be left to mere diplomats, politicians, and business leaders. They have done the best they could, no doubt. But this is an age for spiritual heroes—a time for men and women to be heroic in their faith and in spiritual character and power. The greatest danger to the Christian church today is that of pitching its message too low.

—Dallas Willard, Philosopher and Teacher

TABLE OF CONTENTS

ACKNOWLEDGMENTS

A SPECIAL THANK-YOU GOES to the Mansfield team. Stephen and Beverly, your insight, attention to detail, storytelling abilities, and writing gifts helped bring the manuscript to life. Thank you for your commitment to this project each step of the way.

Thank you to our friends at Charisma for believing in *Focus on the Future*. What an amazing team of leaders and influencers, led by Stephen Strang. Lucy, Debbie, Margarita, Melissa, and SueLee, you all have outdone yourselves once again! We love working with you.

We are indebted to Dina Jones, Kyle Sutton, and Garrett Hedrick for their diligence and commitment to excellence every step of the way through the development of the manuscript and promotion strategies. A special shout out goes to each team member at the American Association of Christian Counselors and the James Dobson Family Institute.

As always, a special thank-you goes to my family for their love and support. Julie, you bring such beauty and light to every day. I am so blessed to be loved by you. To my daughter, Megan; my son-in-law, Ben; and our first granddaughter, Olivia—and to my son, Zach, and his new bride, Evelyn—what joy you all have brought to me. I am overjoyed to be your dad and papa. I don't want to miss or waste a moment of life together. Let's leave it all on the field. Love ya!

FOREWORD

E VERY GREAT REFORMATION begins with an analysis of what is. Focusing on understanding contemporary culture, its history and present state, leads to deciding the best road into the future. The future is inevitable. What we do in the present, as a nation and as individuals, will greatly impact what the future looks like. This book, written by Dr. Tim Clinton, is a well-researched picture of the present state of the family, the church, and philosophical views in contemporary culture. However, the heart of the book focuses on how to move from where we are to where we want to be.

Obviously views differ greatly on what the future should look like. No one denies that we are a greatly divided nation. Not only are we divided, but we have also developed a war-like attitude toward those who disagree with us. Years ago sociologists described our nation as an "argumentative culture," but today we have moved beyond argument and are now seeking to denigrate and destroy those who hold a different view.

The Christian church finds itself in the midst of a secular culture, which leans more toward hate than love. Hate seeks to destroy. Love seeks to enrich. The art of solving conflicts by empathetic listening, with a view to understanding each other's thoughts and feelings, and focusing on finding a solution has been lost. We now focus on winning an argument rather than seeking a solution. What we have failed to note is that when we win an argument, the other person has lost. No one wants to be a loser. So why would we want to create losers, in the family, in church, or in society?

How do we learn to have a win-win solution for our differences? I believe the answer lies in the words of Jesus, who said, "Love your enemies and pray for those who persecute you....Do good to those who hate you" (Matt. 5:43; Luke 6:27, NIV). Who among us can practice this high standard? I believe the answer is, none of us without divine help. That is why those who are truly followers of Christ must take the lead in demonstrating love to those with whom we disagree. Speaking the truth in love is not always easy, but for the Christian it is an imperative. We must treat all humans with dignity and respect. We believe that all humans have worth because they are made in the image of God. In becoming channels of God's love, we can play a redemptive role in impacting the future.

The family is the most basic unit of society. Healthy families tend to produce healthy adults. Healthy churches will focus on the power of Christ to enable husbands and wives to have loving, supportive, caring marriages, which in turn provide a healthy environment for children.

In this book Dr. Tim Clinton not only identifies where we are as a society but points the way to a better future. He shares practical ideas on building healthy families and healthy churches. It is a resource for pastors, counselors, and any Christian who wants to have a positive impact on the future of our world.

—Gary D. Chapman, PhD
Author, *The 5 Love Languages*

WHAT'S PAST IS PROLOGUE

I T WAS A scene of horror that made men's hearts fail them. Jerusalem, with the holy temple within her, was besieged by Babylonian armies. The onslaught lasted for nearly two years. Starvation was rampant, and cannibalism became commonplace. There are accounts of mothers going mad with hunger and consuming their young. Agonies of every kind filled the ancient city.

Finally, in 587 BC the forces of Nebuchadnezzar II broke through Jerusalem's walls and conquered the Holy City. Horrors mounted upon horrors as enemies decimated the city and pillaged the sacred temple, sending precious metals back to their homeland. The Babylonians forced King Zedekiah to watch them kill his sons. Then, they blinded him and sent him to Babylon. More than four thousand of his people were taken into captivity with him. Only a poor and destitute few remained as a remnant in the land with nothing but carnage and rubble.

The inevitable question swirling in the minds of the captives as they trudged their way to bondage in Babylon was, Why?

The prophet Jeremiah bore witness to all these events. He too pondered and grieved and sought his God for answers. Finally, in the Book of Lamentations, he wrote the words that explained the terrible destruction of God's people. Jerusalem, he warned, "did not consider her future," so "her fall was astounding."[1]

FACING DIFFICULT TIMES

In many ways, America has been on the same trajectory as Israel in Jeremiah's day. What's more, I believe that the pandemic and the presidential election of 2020 have caused unprecedented changes in the fabric of our country. Overnight our lives turned upside down, and the tone of our nation changed. As we emerge from these events, we are wondering what the future holds for our health, our jobs, our food supply, and our safety. Beyond this, many wonder about the long-term economic effect and how these things will play out on a global scale. What we experienced was not only an outbreak of sickness from the virus but also an outbreak of fear and anxiety.

God and His Word are the antidotes. Christian organizations have continued to provide supplies and services to the communities hit the hardest. As individuals and families navigate the return to social normalcy, they are reevaluating their priorities and lifestyles.

It's a good reminder that we can have faith that overcomes fear in troubled times. Psalm 46 is a favorite of mine. Many people turn to it for encouragement in dark times when things seem hopeless. Let's look at the first three verses:

> God is our refuge and strength, a very present help in trouble. Therefore we will not fear, even though the earth be removed, and though the mountains be carried into the midst of the sea; though its waters roar and be troubled, though the mountains shake with its swelling.
>
> —PSALM 46:1–3, NKJV

God is in the midst of our troubled times. If we call on Him, He can bring peace to our situation. Verses 3–9 of Psalm 46 remind us that no matter what we are facing, God is in the midst of it. And then the psalm says,

> Be still, and know that I am God; I will be exalted among the nations, I will be exalted in the earth! The LORD of hosts is with us; the God of Jacob is our refuge.
> —PSALM 46:10–11, NKJV

By the time you read this book, the social distancing of early 2020 may be well behind us, but the repercussions might still be rippling throughout the land. Whatever season we're facing as you read this, we can hold tenaciously to Psalm 46 and reclaim our voices as one nation under God. The times we are living in are truly momentous. As Christians, we have the answers the world is looking for, solutions that can change the course of our nation. As we focus on the future, don't let it overwhelm you. There is hope, and one person can make a difference. This book offers insights on what you can do to impact our generation and leave a legacy for your children. This is a moment we cannot overlook. We cannot miss the opportunity to step into the fight for our family, faith, and freedoms. We can—and, I believe, will—win this fight one family, one mom, one dad, one day at a time. Regaining our voice and reclaiming the ground we've recently lost are crucial in this hour.

AMERICA AND THE ROMAN EMPIRE

To help illustrate the critical point we've reached as a nation, let me ask you to think back to the world into which the Christian church was born, the world of the Roman Empire. It was a time marked by confusion and fear.

Imagine a world in which the emperor is considered a god but dozens of other gods also rule daily life. Imagine a religion-weary people who are often confused about what god to honor so a child will be born healthy, a crop will flourish, or a voyage will go well. These were the Roman people. They were tyrannized by the demands of religions and priests, by the complicated system of deities thrust upon them.

Then consider the sheer violence of the time. People were burned to death and eaten by wild animals and tortured for the entertainment of crowds. Criminals were whipped and crucified, all in public view. It was a brutal age when it was acceptable for the elderly to commit suicide and fathers could decide not to accept newborn babies as members of their families.[2] And I haven't even touched on the shocking, rampant sexual perversion.

I could go on, but why have I taken the time to describe these things? Because there was an answer for it all. It came in the birth of the Messiah in a manger in Bethlehem and then the birth of the Christian church on the day of Pentecost decades later. As that early church grew and began to address the crises of Roman society, God granted a traumatized people His love and healing and wholeness.

The people of God offered a sick and suffering society a better way. We know from the pages of Roman history that the Christians began to care for the discarded and abandoned. The churches gathered abandoned babies and children. They cared for the elderly and the sick. They also won the Roman people to Christ in high numbers and began to teach them of the value of each person in God's eyes and the vital role of the godly family.[3]

The early church was a countercultural movement. Believers fought to end the infanticide and sexual perversion that had tortured the empire. They almost wiped out these practices.[4] The apostle Paul told the Corinthians to conduct courts of their own rather than take their disputes to secular judges.[5] The early believers obeyed. Soon it became known that the best place for justice was these Christian courts.[6] Justice spread. The wisdom of God came into public view. Kindness and mercy prevailed. It was nothing short of amazing.

The hardness lifted progressively. The coldness in human relationships abated. Men and women heard in the preaching of the gospel how they ought to conduct themselves, what power God had given them for doing good. Actions changed. Words changed. New customs came into being. Life became sacred and protected for millions of the Roman people. Awareness grew of the soul as the place where God lived in a person, as a holy place to be treated with love.

In fact, it is not going too far to say that love won. The brutal, soul-trouncing Roman Empire gave way to a Christian message rooted in human worth and the soul's value. It wasn't perfect, and it wasn't the same everywhere. Yet the Christian message made such a difference that Roman rulers started handing authority for civil matters to pastors and churches, so effective had they been in changing lives.[7] A kingdom perspective, kingdom culture, and kingdom mindset healed the hearts and minds of the people.

My goal is to encourage you with this review of how the Christian faith changed the Roman Empire and with the fact that we in America today are not Rome. We do not have it nearly as bad. But we are similar in that we are heading toward Roman levels of chaos and violence. We can exhibit Roman levels of disregard for the weak and infirm. We see a nearly equal level of sexual perversion. We are witnessing rampant sexual abuse, the horrors of late-term abortion, and even infanticide. We are seeing much the same kind of attack on the family. The souls of people are ground up in our callous and abusive age, just as they were in ancient and pagan Rome.

But here's the good news: What changed history once can do

it again. What saved a society two millennia ago can do it today. This is why we've met together over these pages. Let's get started!

CHAPTER 1

THE REPRIEVE

T HE FUTURE. OUR days will inevitably fold into continual tomorrows until we leave this earth. Though time moving forward is unavoidable, the future still feels mysterious and daunting. Yet wise people have the courage and foresight to ponder the future. They imagine what might unfold, how the days to come might be, and what steps they must take in preparation. They map out careful plans. They make the changes needed to face or to change what is coming. They do all they can to fashion the kind of future they would hope for future generations.

Thinking about the future in this way has led to much of the greatness we see in history. The visionary spirit of our American Founding Fathers is at the core of our rich legacy. It is why their speeches and private letters brim with references to posterity, with expressions of their hopes for generations yet unborn. John Adams captured this well when he wrote in a letter to his wife, "Posterity! you will never know how much it cost the present generation to preserve your freedom! I hope you will make a good use of it."[1]

It is also what Abraham Lincoln did. When he declared in his epic speech at Gettysburg that "government of the people, by the people, for the people, shall not perish from the earth," he was thinking of the future, of what that moment meant for the good of the world to come. His words have been quoted the world over, especially where brave people long to see good government ruling a just and prosperous nation they can pass proudly to their children.

We saw the same forward-focused direction in Dr. Martin Luther King Jr. In his famous "I Have a Dream" speech, he spoke of a future, of a dream that "one day this nation will rise up, live out the true meaning of its creed: 'We hold these truths to be self-evident, that all men are created equal.'" It was a dream yet unfulfilled when Dr. King spoke it, and it is yet unfulfilled today, but it was promised by our forefathers and intended by many great souls who came before us. Because of Dr. King's words, a generation has reached for his dream of the future and has increasingly made it a reality.

Considering the future is a common trait among the whole-hearted, among people of faith, among people of God and godly vision—the exceptional and everyday heroes. They stand in their moment in time, however troubled, and they face the call of the future. They envision what can be and how to answer the challenges of their age. Then they build for a future better than the past they have known.

This is exactly the opportunity we have now. I believe our generation has a mandate to focus on the future. I believe our voices matter now more than ever. There's been an agenda to silence our voices, and we'll look at what has led to that. We'll also discuss why it's urgent to get that voice back—the future of our faith, our families, and our freedom depends on it.

Our Moment in Time

We all know that we are living in a tumultuous age. Our society is in upheaval. Our nation is torn. As a result, our nation's political landscape is largely unfruitful. We have dissension and strife in nearly every arena, on almost every topic of importance. Contention reigns and is growing. Disillusionment is spreading, and a divide is deepening in our country. Yet a resilient American spirit—something deep inside our hearts, the substance our country was founded on—is beginning to reemerge. It appears as an uprising of hope, of hard work, and of the courage we need to heal our nation.

Some believe we are in a critical moment in which Christianity and conservative values must be fought for like never before in the United States. I couldn't agree more. Our nation continues to move at breakneck speed into relativism, hedonism, and a rejection of the values of human life and family. Regardless of who sits in the Oval Office, we should no longer wait for government to set the tone of respecting and honoring the stalwart values of Christian and social conservatism.

In addition, researchers are exposing the dysfunction and destruction of modern-day issues such as pornography and absentee fathers while also finding the positive outcomes of faith-based living. We are witnesses to unprecedented events that beckon observers to stop and stare in awe at the political, cultural, and emotional landscape of our times. Yet our future depends on our ability to quickly assess and move forward, ever fighting for our future. There is no time to gape at the wreckage or the new risings of hope. Every called warrior must show up for battle.

Our marching orders are not simply a matter of policy. We will take action on many fronts, guided by fervent prayer. I believe that Dallas Willard's words aptly describe our times: "Social and political revolutions have shown no tendency to transform the heart of darkness that lies deep in the breast of every human being....Obviously, the problem *is* a spiritual one. And so must be the cure."[2]

This reprieve gives us a brief moment to ponder our circumstances and bravely put our convictions to action, doing what heroic people have always done as they look to the future. Years ago, someone asked religious scholar Martin Marty if he believed the current spirituality surge in America was real. His response caught my attention. He said, "The hunger is always authentic.... It's just that you can feed it with Twinkies or with broccoli."[3] By that, he meant that *it all depends on what the church does with the opportunity culture has given to her.* Think about that. Let those words sink in.

A number of years ago, I attended a meeting with Dr. James Dobson at the headquarters of Focus on the Family in Colorado Springs. I do not remember the reason for the meeting, but I do remember his challenging words. In a 2017 Family Talk newsletter, Dr. Dobson recalled that same meeting and said, "We need to pray that the church will awaken and take her rightful place. Until then, parachurch organizations must stand in the gap—but we must pray that the church be awakened."[4]

> Our true hope is the power of Christ coming alive in His body, the church. The question is, What will the church do with the opportunity culture is giving us right now? #focusonthefuture

Pastor Rick Warren once reminded me that the one social institution in every community across the globe is the church. Our true hope is the power of Christ coming alive in His body, the church. The question is, What will the church do with the opportunity culture is giving us right now? Could it be that, like Esther, we have been called "for such a time as this"?[5] We must focus on the future and seek to discover our part in leaving a legacy that will impact future generations.

To do this, we must first confront the truth about our nation as it is today. We must be courageous, clear-eyed, and willing to know the facts, however disturbing they may be. Only then can we be the change our hoped-for future requires.

As Christians, we need to show sincere compassion while we fight for responsible solutions to control threats to our national safety. We must follow our call as Christians to love mercy *and* act justly[6] rather than adopt a response that is only merciful or only just. We must clearly explain and put into enthusiastic action our responsibility to care for those in need.

Rita Dunaway writes in *Restoring America's Soul*, "If we fail to describe and explain our own vision for caring for the poor, sick, and elderly, then we create a vacuum for the Left to fill with their assumptions that we are simply greedy, tight-fisted, or too concerned with our own selfish pursuits to consider the unfortunate plights of others. If we allow these assumptions to go unchallenged, then we are perpetuating a fundamental misunderstanding about who we are and what our ideology is."[7]

When we give in to assumptions about the ideas of others or do not make our ideology clear, we are participating in a lack of communication that tears down what needs to be restored. We get into a place where we can't even reason together. Even more, we can no longer hear each other.

My American Story

I want to tell you a bit about my own story so you know why I feel so strongly about the things I've said here. In many ways, I had a traditional, all-American childhood. The main difference from others of my generation, perhaps, is that my family was deeply Christian. Beyond this, my life was relatively normal. I grew up in rural Pennsylvania, less than an hour north of Altoona, and I was one of eight children.

My father was the kindest man I've ever known. He was the pastor of three small-town churches, a circuit rider of sorts who tended small churches and groups of Christians throughout our region of Pennsylvania. My father was also deeply patriotic. As kids, we heard the heroic tales of our forebears often.

Dad was one of those World War II veterans that Tom Brokaw called the "greatest generation" ever. He talked about being on the USS *Pennsylvania* in the South Pacific and his war experiences as a young man. He was so happy to get back home that he kissed the ground when he finally arrived stateside. My dad was thankful to God that he came back home at all, unlike many who gave the ultimate sacrifice during that horrific war. It just made sense then that the Fourth of July was one of his favorite holidays and that he continued to fly a flag in the yard until the day God took him home.

The deep kindness I saw in my dad was probably the fruit of his deep faith. He believed that God was real and that His ways could be understood and lived by faithful people. Dad never browbeat. He was never harsh but instead taught an intelligent, peaceful faith born of the certainty that God called him to serve and was with him. When Dad died, I stood in line with my siblings for hours, listening to those he loved and served share how much he meant to them. I've often thought of how his impact on their lives will move down through generations in ways that only heaven can record.

I surprise people by telling them that Dad never raised a hand to me. He always reasoned. He always explained. You respected him and never wanted to disappoint him. He had power and authority by virtue of his character and his way. It was how he shaped his children.

However, my mother was another story. Now, she too was kind and loving and loved to laugh, but she had no hesitation about disciplining her children. She was old-school! To her, a spanking was love applied to the seat of understanding, and she had much love to apply. Steadfast in her convictions, she raised us to stand strong in what we believed.

So, we had a relatively typical small-town American life together as a family. Jesus was at the heart of our lives. We honored and understood that my father's pastoral work required sacrifice. We gave ourselves to school, sports, friends, and the rites of passage of most American children of our time. Parenting does matter, and my parents made such a deep imprint on my soul in my early years that when an eleventh-grade teacher once asked me what I wanted to do one day, I replied that I wanted to be in ministry like my father.

An interesting twist for me, however, was that I developed a fascination with the ways of human nature earlier than most people. I suppose this was due to my father's work, my large family, my parents' deep connections to other people, and, I realize now, the calling of God on my own life. I wouldn't have expressed it this way at the time, but all these years later, I see my early ponderings in this light.

Several defining moments in my early years served to set this trajectory. A pivotal moment happened when I was sixteen. I remember that I had hurt my knee during preseason high school football, and I was home waiting to go to a checkup for my injury. While I was still in bed that morning, the phone rang, and my dad answered. That is when he received the news that my sister Candace had been in a horrible car accident.

I recall vividly that my father and I rushed to the scene. When we arrived, we saw the mangled car and my unconscious, bloodied sister inside. On an old dirt road, I slammed the car in park, jumped out, and started running for her. It was typical of my father's nature that he immediately said, "Tim, you go to her, and I'll pray."

I ran to the car. The scene was ghastly, but I climbed in and began checking my sister.

"She has a pulse!" I shouted to Dad.

"Work on her, and I'll keep praying," he replied.

I remember green gum was all through her teeth. I did what I could for Candy, and then we got her in an ambulance and to a hospital. She suffered a traumatic brain injury and then was comatose for nearly thirty days. It was a torturous time of waiting and hoping and praying, but I clearly remember that my family's hope was in God, and that hope, while tested, never wavered.

An episode like this makes an impression on a young man's soul. It changes him. It teaches that life is delicate, that it can be taken away. Life is precious and should be respected and lovingly protected. It also reveals the condition of the human soul. He sees faith in action. He sees parents facing the possible death of a child. He sees courage arising and hearts reaching for hope and what people mean in each other's lives as family and community responding to trouble. He witnesses God working through love and tender care and the gifts He has given to human beings.

Today, my sister is married with three children. We call her Ruthie Graham because she is always evangelizing and singing God's praises. She had a long road of recovery from her traumatic brain injury and still struggles with chronic pain and the trauma effects. It has only made her more thankful for the gift of life—and us thankful for her. My sister's car accident taught me much and marked my young life. I'll never forget August 20, 1976.

Another incident also impacted me profoundly. There was a man in our church whom we all knew fairly well. He was a good man so far as I knew, and he was a friend of my father's. One night he found his wife with another man. He shot that man and killed him. He then called and talked to my father, who was deeply grieved and encouraged him to turn himself in. Perhaps you can imagine the questions stirring in my teenage mind. How can a man murder someone? What kind of pain in the human heart drives him to do it?

The whole episode moved me to spend long hours pondering the human condition. I wanted to understand what drives behavior. I desired to find the keys to helping people with their inner challenges, with having good relationships and a heart of peace and faith, which I had learned from my father was the source of a happy life.

I was challenged and inspired in this fledgling search by what was going on in our society. I grew up during the 1960s and 1970s, a time when our culture was in upheaval. We often focus on the tearing of the social fabric during that time and the stunning political and social events that marked the age. Yet I wondered about what was happening to the human soul. What moved people to the kinds of violence we saw in those decades—assassinations, riots, home invasions, police brutality, and war? What vacuum in the heart drove the young to throw themselves into the excesses of the sexual revolution and embrace every perversion masquerading as pleasure? Why was this generation so eager to discard the ways of their ancestors and seek out novel alternatives to marriage, family, child-rearing, and relationships as a whole? Why were so many, particularly the young, in such torment of soul, in such agony of heart? All these questions filled my mind and stirred me even more fiercely in my desire to understand the inner life of human beings.

During high school, I enlisted in the US Army Reserve. Right after graduation, I attended boot camp and advanced infantry training at Fort Sill, Oklahoma. Then I made my way home to work and to try to save some money to attend college. All the usual questions about what I would do next faced me. I was fortunate. As these questions began to crescendo in my life, I received a golden opportunity. Just then, I came upon some news that would change the direction of my life.

Dr. Jerry Falwell, a courageous and outspoken pastor on our national scene, had founded Lynchburg Baptist College, which was renamed Liberty Baptist College in 1976. One of his convictions was that the children of pastors would attend the school with reduced tuition. This was a stunning act of generosity on his part and the school as a whole. For me, the son of a small-town pastor and one of eight children, the chance to go to college was like a gift from heaven.

I packed my bags and left for Virginia. The experience has shaped me ever since. I decided to major in pastoral ministry and minor in biblical Greek, later adding a double minor in counseling. Not only did I receive a fabulous education and build lifetime friendships at Liberty, but I also met the love of my life, Julie. We have lived a glorious adventure in the decades since, but it all began on the Liberty campus.

While driving a car, when we look in the rearview mirror, the scene is condensed. So it is with how we remember our lives. It all seems compacted somehow, even automatic.

I wanted to attend Dallas Theological Seminary for my graduate work, but I decided to remain at Liberty University and earn a master's in counseling. My questions about what drives human nature and how I could help to heal the souls of people fueled my studies. I later taught at Liberty. I started a counseling service called Light Counseling near the university and began to see people get free from the inner bondages that held them. In time, I had the wonderful opportunity to earn my doctorate at the historic College of William and Mary in Williamsburg, Virginia.

The years that followed were busy, but I thrived on the ministry God was allowing me to have. I eventually taught thousands of students at Liberty. My life's passion was surfacing. We lived in a damaging, wounding world. Still, God loved people and was always reaching to them with compassion. In addition, His Scriptures and His ways held the keys for health in the human soul, for the relationships intended to make life full and rich and meaningful. These were the pillars of my work, as they are now.

God had plans for my life that would have overwhelmed me in my early days had I any hint of them. I had long dreamed of a worldwide association of counselors that would encourage a biblical approach to helping people get well. Amazingly, the day would come when I would lead the American Association of Christian Counselors, the largest and most diverse faith-based mental health organization in the world.

In telling you about my life, I yearn for you to see that I keenly feel the devastation of our modern world. As I've described, we are living at a time when souls are traumatized, when inner wounds torment millions, when suicide and addiction are rampant, and when hurting people hurt others through abuse and abandonment. The pandemic and modern-day experiences have only heightened the mental health crisis in our land. We are now witnessing a mental health disaster, especially among our youths. Answers exist. Healing, health, and happiness are to be had. There is hope in Christ! We need bold believers who ponder this moment in time, consider the future, and courageously storm into that future armed with the knowledge and skills their generation yearns for.

I want to encourage you about what is possible in our

generation. The truth of God's Word can save a society. It will simply take people with an uncommon level of devotion. People of faith. People of God. People who understand the sanctity of life, the divine purpose for every person, and the glory of the family as God has ordained it. If these types of people will make use of the moment we find ourselves in now, if we come together, stand together, and storm into our age with purpose, we can have an impact. Our country needs us to make a difference. Our children need it. The future of Christianity in America depends on it.

We have to know our times. We have to step into this moment in history, this graciously given reprieve. We have to consider the future. Then we need to take healing to our troubled generation.

CHAPTER 2

HOPE FOR OUR
TROUBLED LAND

I T'S BEEN SAID that to know where you're going, you must first look at where you've been. For many Americans of faith, for people of traditional values and godly purpose, nearly everything we hold dear about American life has been under increasing attack for the past sixty years. This is primarily due to the left-leaning influencers of American culture.

In short, Christianity has been under assault. In truth, our beliefs, our faith culture, and even our hopes for our country have been targeted by a vast majority of those in Hollywood, the news media, the education system, and the government.

As this agenda has unfolded and taken hold of the minds of an entire generation, Americans of traditional values have seen themselves losing the culture war with little or no hope of a turning point anytime soon. The United States has become "progressively more hostile to Christian civilization."[1] The fallout can be seen in every facet of our society.

VIOLENCE ON THE RISE

It's not an exaggeration to say that America is a traumatized nation. Not only has the nation's downward spiral affected us politically. It has impacted us in the most personal and individual ways. In 2018 an estimated 678,000 victims of child maltreatment were discovered by state officials.[2] Every 73 seconds, an American is sexually assaulted.[3] On average, nearly twenty people per minute are physically abused by an intimate partner in the United States. During one year, this equates to more than ten million women and men.[4] Some 12 percent of women in the United States have difficulty getting or staying pregnant.[5] The issues run the gamut, and too many people in our country are going through life either numbing themselves or reacting to pain they don't know what to do with. These people are our neighbors, and we need to step into their distress if we are going to fight for our nation.

> Too many people in our country are going through life either numbing themselves or reacting to pain they don't know what to do with. These people are our neighbors, and we need to step into their distress if we are going to fight for our nation. #focusonthefuture

Too many Americans have experienced violence and trauma at the hands of others. "In the decade between 2009 and 2018, 1,121 Americans were killed and 836 more were wounded in 194 mass shootings, with an average of 19 shootings each year. Among the casualties were 309 children and teens killed and 194 more wounded, as well as 19 law enforcement officers killed and 23 wounded. These numbers are staggering, yet they represent just a small portion of the lives forever changed after a mass shooting shakes a community with terror and grief."[6]

We are losing individuals and families to mental health issues and generational patterns that could be helped with education and counseling. Nothing reveals this like the stunning rise in suicide we are experiencing in our time, especially since the COVID-19 pandemic.

The American people today are dying by suicide in higher numbers than at any time since the Great Depression and World War II. The suicide rate has risen 33 percent since 1999, with 2017 having the "highest age-adjusted suicide rate" since 1942. The facts concealed within these trends are equally disturbing. Usually, men commit suicide more than women. Yet since 1999, female suicide rates have risen by 53 percent compared with 26 percent for men.[7]

The breakdown of suicide rates by age is also heartbreaking. Among adults, "the most suicide deaths are reported among people ages 45 to 64." Yet tragically, among youth, the suicide rates of boys and girls ages ten to fourteen have increased more rapidly than among any other age group. The ethnic breakdown of suicide rates is also troubling. While every ethnic group saw a jump in suicides from 1999 to 2017, the rates were the highest among American Indians and Alaska natives.[8]

Equally dispiriting are some of the reasons behind these increases in suicide rates. Though experts say that the whole subject is complicated, they often point first to the opioid crisis. In every age range and ethnicity, opioid use is known to drive suicidal behavior among users. The number of suicides rises not only among those who take the drugs but also among their family members and friends. In fact, opioid use affects the mental health of entire communities. As a biomedical informatics expert at Harvard Medical School reports, heavy opioid use in a region means that "the entire community is bleeding. Kids see less of a future, they see more of their friends dying."[9]

Aside from drug use, one of the most significant factors in suicide rates is loneliness, especially since the pandemic. With the breakdown of the American family and social structure and with social media giving us the illusion of intimacy without the reality, people are increasingly finding themselves painfully alone. The great lockdown of 2020 with the dawn of social distancing isolated us even more. While many families found each other, others lost their sense of connectedness. And the desperate need for human relationships has now soared. Almost immediately we saw an uptick in alcohol consumption and abuse. In fact, the Associated Press reported that alcohol sales increased by 55 percent the week of March 15–21, 2020.[10]

About 45 percent of Americans now say that this new normal has affected their mental health.[11] I will add that it has affected their relational health too. People being locked down in nursing homes with no visitors and dying alone in hospitals is a tragedy their surviving loved ones will not easily forget. Many have experienced lost dreams, lost jobs, and lost loved ones.

Even more, the pace, pressure, and pain of everyday life are spilling over into anger, resentment, and bitterness that show up in bullying and almost terroristic ways on social media. Often it proves too much for victims. When experts do the psychological postmortems on suicide deaths, they find that sheer isolation can be a key factor.[12] Social isolation can lead people to think, "No one is close enough to me to care. I've lost everyone. No one even knows I'm alive. Maybe I shouldn't be." A columnist for the *Washington Post* has simply concluded, "Suicide rates are at an all-time high. We need hope more than ever."[13]

I've mentioned the opioid epidemic as a factor in rising suicide rates. That's because it's personal for almost every American.

Virtually everyone I talk to knows someone who is addicted. Between 2006 and 2012, almost 100,000 deaths were caused by the prescription opioid epidemic. This fact is painful enough. Yet we also now know that "America's largest drug companies saturated the country with more than 76 billion oxycodone and hydrocodone pain pills" during this same time.[14] In other words, while the death rate was rising, cynical corporations were making the crisis worse by dumping dangerous pills on the market for profit.

The callousness of these corporations makes this whole epidemic even more wounding to our national soul. As people were dying, the number of pills shoved onto the market surged. In 2006, the number of dangerous pills was about 8.4 billion. But by 2012, that number had increased to 12.6 billion—an astonishing 51 percent increase in six years. No demographic has gone untouched by the opioid crisis, either through prescribed pills or nonmedical opioid use. Many of our kids—the star quarterback, the teenage prom queen, the quiet girl next door—have become victims.[15]

There are now lawsuits and government investigations pursuing justice here. Yet the traumatic fact remains that to some individuals and organizations profits often matter more than human lives—and people die. Deaths from both opioid use and related suicides have skyrocketed. We can understand how knowledge of this has hardened Americans, how it has made us less trusting and more cynical of government, of corporations, and even of the medical community that is meant to heal and not to do harm.

AMERICA AND THE FAMILY

Pope John Paul II once wrote, "As the family goes, so goes the nation, and so goes the whole world."[16] I agree. The family is under such a strong attack today. Some of this, of course, is simply a matter of human sin and irresponsibility. Absent fathers, divorce, and disconnection often result from mere selfishness. But there is a real anti-family agenda stridently opposed to the traditional family, the institution that has been a bulwark of so much human progress and achievement, a haven of all that is essential to healthy and thriving human beings. God has ordained the family to be an anchor where hearts and hands are fashioned to grow, love, and be loved.

Without vital, loving families, people are without belonging, without support of any kind, and without the loving connections that make for healthy souls who can sustain the blows of this life. We will examine this much more closely in the pages to come. For now, suffice it to say that the deterioration of the American family is the source of nearly every symptom of cultural decline, from criminal activity to plunging academic performances, from damaged mental health to poor physical health, from rising poverty to shredded social networks.

Virtually every facet of culture has been force-feeding our families a steady diet of trendy, left-leaning social change. A particular shock to many Americans was the relentless efforts and ability of LGBTQ advocates to position those who identify themselves as part of the homosexual community as a minority group to be prioritized, protected, and eventually revered. This was mainly done through the media normalizing and then celebrating homosexual relationships—often to age groups too young to be contemplating any type of sexuality at all.

AMERICA AND THE CHURCH

Next to the attacks on family, today we are experiencing strident opposition to the church. Here again, society often attacks the very institutions that meet its desperate needs. This comes home to me every time a massive disaster hits in the United States. Whether it is a flood, a hurricane, an act of terrorism, a pandemic, or some other trauma that leaves hurting people in its wake, what do we always see afterward? Churches show up in force. Disaster areas are flooded by church vans and buses and legions of church members moving out in love and generosity to make a difference.

How is it, then, that society sees churches as a threat? Why the church shootings? Why the culture of animosity toward the Christian gospel? Why the government policies restricting religion and religious expression in American society? The battle and concerns over religious liberty when the pandemic hit were staggering. We should remember that the churches are a hedge against the immoral behavior so destructive to society. It is the churches that call for social justice and individual responsibility. It is the churches that sponsor every kind of social service from feeding centers to after-school learning programs, from ministries to prisoners to care for the immigrant and the downtrodden.

Perhaps part of the opposition to churches is an inadequate understanding of what the church is and does. Rita Dunaway writes, "If conservatives hope to recapture the hearts and minds of America, we must *communicate* this reason to the masses. We must effectively communicate *our* plan for caring for 'the least of these' and for spurring our society toward what is good, true, and beautiful."[17]

Perhaps another reason for the opposition to churches in America is that they bring conviction. Could it be that churches remind Americans of God and His claim on their lives? Is it that churches hold up a righteous mirror to a sin-sick society? Is it that they call for standards in an age of license, God's order in an age without moral restraint?

Are there concerns with the church? Yes. There have always been debates, unrest, division, and concern over toxic faith. In a lot of ways, the church has ignored or is ignoring many issues, challenges, and concerns. Tragically, some church leadership has fueled divisions and even hurt those they serve. The recent child sexual abuse allegation crisis has raised concern about care, counsel, and ministry in the twenty-first century. Psychologist and trauma expert Diane Langberg believes that the church needs to look more like Christ than an institution.

AMERICA AND ENTITLEMENT

Tragically, we live in an age of ingratitude, in the era of the ungrateful American. Though we are among the most blessed people who have ever lived, many Americans today feel that they have been cheated and that nothing is coming from their nation or their ancestors for which they should be thankful. It's hard to believe, but even socialism has become enticing to many who know very little of the realities of this evil system.

Some Americans share feelings of anger and disrespect for our country. Though they live in the safest and most opportunity-filled nation on earth, they despise its history, its institutions, its traditions, and its values.

What they rage against is not just the human forces that created this nation but also, I believe, the divine care that has always been at the heart of the American experience. No one expressed this better than Abraham Lincoln, who, on March 30, 1863, rebuked his generation for the same ingratitude that is a rising force today:

> But we have forgotten God. We have forgotten the gracious hand which preserved us in peace, and multiplied and enriched and strengthened us; and we have vainly imagined, in the deceitfulness of our hearts, that all these blessings were produced by some superior wisdom and virtue of our own.[18]

Struggling to turn to God for the healing and restoration we so desperately need, we instead choose to rage against the past and one another. This becomes an excuse for inaction. Rather than strive for true racial harmony, some rage only against statues, demanding that all images of our founders be removed from public spaces. Rather than take action to fight the poverty that besets every age and nation, some of our peers blame the free-market system. Rather than striving to understand the thinking and sacrifices of Americans who went before them, radicals have highjacked the real issues for nothing more than political purposes. It sometimes seems as if the people of this generation overlook the counsel of the past.

Yet there is hope, and in this God-ordained season for considering our ways and our future, there is much reason to believe that we can forge a better future. This ought to and can be a time of determination to repair and rebuild, to heal and focus on the future now.

CHAPTER 3

THE NEW BATTLE
FOR THE FAMILY

I CANNOT THINK OF the words *battle for the family* without thinking of Dr. James Dobson. There was a time in my life when I would have been thrilled just to sit and hear him speak. I'm honored to say that today he has become a friend, a man at whose side I'm privileged to serve. Always he has been a modern-day champion of faith, family, and freedom; a mentor; and an example of a godly husband and father.

Dr. Dobson's book *Dare to Discipline* first appeared in 1970 as a fresh wind of wisdom to our times. Allow me to describe what the scene was then. The tumultuous decade of the 1960s had just ended, with all its rejection of traditional ways and its headlong rush into anything new, trendy, antiestablishment, and, frankly, non-Christian. We were still embroiled in the Vietnam War, Richard Nixon was president, and the counterculture was at high tide.

The pivotal Woodstock festival had occurred only the year before. So had the ghastly Tate-LaBianca murders, engineered and led by Charles Manson. And in December 1969, a member of the Hells Angels motorcycle gang murdered a black man at a concert while the Rolling Stones sang "Under My Thumb." In 1970, the cultural revolution continued to turn ugly. Jimi Hendrix died, Janis Joplin died, and the Beatles broke up. As disturbing as all of this was, the sexual revolution was challenging the role of the traditional family nationwide.

Then came James Dobson. He was not just another transient voice in an unstable age. He had earned his PhD in child development from the University of Southern California and had served on the faculty of the medical school there for many years. He also served on staff at the Children's Hospital of Los Angeles. Added to all this experience was his great depth as a Christian. His father was a traveling evangelist and pastor for the Church of the Nazarene. "Jimmy," as James was called then, enjoyed a closeness with his father and yearned to develop the same type of relationship with God that he saw in his dad.[1] Rather than feeling a draw into full-time ministry, however, James Dobson felt the call to become a Christian psychologist.[2]

We should pause to consider how radical this was. At that time in history, some Christians believed psychology to be a rival religion to faith in Jesus Christ. Most psychologists were secular, and some psychological schools of thought treated religion with disdain and even hostility. Many professional psychologists or psychiatrists had long before discarded any belief in God and so came to see religion as "a type of cognitive error that is said to have harmful cognitive...and emotional...consequences."[3] Modern psychology represented an entirely different value system from Christianity. As Professor Paul Vitz of New York University wrote, the religion of modern psychology was one in which "the commandment 'Know and express thyself' has replaced the Judeo-Christian commandment 'Love God and others.'"[4]

Dr. Dobson thought he saw another way. As he read Scripture, he saw not only God's saving work in Jesus Christ for all the world but also God's truths for the health and healing of the human soul. In fact, in studying psychology and practicing as a psychologist, he often confronted problems that were described along with their solutions in the Bible. In other words, Dr. Dobson came to believe that it was possible to use both the insights of psychology and the revelation of Scripture to heal souls and build healthy lives and families.

Our baffled age was ready for such wisdom, and that's why *Dare to Discipline* won such a vast readership. People began to see that biblical truth for human conduct and relationships was relevant, practical, and transforming. A hunger for more led to the founding of Focus on the Family in 1977, with its flagship radio broadcast by the same name.

I wonder if Dr. Dobson's voice on that radio program meant to you what it did to so many millions. In an increasingly fatherless, unreasonable, unrooted age, Dr. Dobson was both prophet and patriarch. He explained our times to us. He helped us understand in simple terms what had gone wrong with our relationships, our marriages, our parenting, and even our schools and how we could recover what had been lost. He decoded our world and then taught us how to apply God's truths to our dysfunctional age and broken lives.

For decades, Dr. Dobson was the wise man on the air who helped to center us again. Yet he did not just teach us about family matters. He also taught us about our Christian heritage in this country. He spoke of the realm of politics and government as something Christians ought to be involved in. He helped to lead the homeschool movement yet also kept speaking wisdom for our nation's public schools. He led the battle against abortion and challenged the rising homosexual agenda of his day. In short, he guided us through our times, pointing out the pitfalls, explaining God's answers, and inspiring us to action in our age, all while calling us to keep our eyes on Jesus.

It is no wonder that in 2005 the *New York Times* called him "the nation's most influential evangelical leader."[5] It is also no wonder that he has advised five presidents, was given nearly every humanitarian and broadcast award possible for him, and is still revered as one of the most important Christian voices in the world—five decades after he first stepped onto the global stage with *Dare to Discipline.*

It is easy to describe a life and influence like Dr. Dobson's and for all of it to seem effortless and inevitable. It wasn't. He experienced great adversity and hardship in his journey. When Dr. Dobson stood forthrightly against the growing pornography industry in our country, pornographers made a film in protest using images of the real James Dobson interspersed with the filthy acts from porn movies. There were also times when opposers threatened his life, protested at his speeches, and vilified him for his stances on moral issues. Even his fellow Christians sometimes attacked him publicly and distanced themselves from his work. I know that difficult seasons always befall the heroic, but I also want us to remember the opposition this valiant man endured and how he stood boldly in the face of it all.

Not long ago, Dr. Dobson received three awards that I thought were very symbolic of his influence on our culture. In 2017, the Faith & Freedom Coalition gave him the Winston Churchill Lifetime Achievement Award. How fitting this was, for James Dobson is indeed a Churchill—warning us, calling us to battle, describing the world as it might be if we returned to God's ways and purposes. In 2016, Arizona Christian University gave him the Daniel Award. He is indeed a Daniel, a man welcomed into the courts of power in our country but also a man determined to speak God's truth whatever the cost, whatever idols have to fall.

In addition, in 2015, the Justice Foundation gave him the Defender of Life Award. This is very much the way I think of James Dobson. The Latin words *Fidei Defensor* have long been used of monarchs and heads of state in Europe. They mean, simply, "Defender of the Faith." This is what Dr. Dobson has done with every breath: defend the Christian faith, defend the implications of that faith in our society, defend the family that faith produces, and defend what is best for the human beings God loves so deeply.

I can tell you as a man who works closely with James Dobson that he is as warm, as genuine, as devoted, and as fierce of purpose in person as he is in public. Though he is always the gentleman you've seen and heard through the years, our generation has given us no finer warrior for God than Dr. Dobson.

THE BATTLE FOR THE FAMILY

Now, I have also said that James Dobson is a prophet, and I do not believe that this is an overstatement. No one has been more prescient about the family, its importance to society, and the reasons it is a target in our generation than Dr. Dobson. We are seeing what he predicted playing out in our country. As I mentioned earlier, the American family is under attack, bombarded from every side: divorce and absentee fathers, the strident radical LGBTQ agenda, encroachment into the family by overreaching government, and even secular philosophies that denigrate the family and seek to reduce its power.

Dan Valentine, long-time columnist for the *Salt Lake Tribune*, once said that "a school is a building of four walls...with tomorrow inside."[6] I believe that, in the same way, a family is a living organism that contains the future of society. This is because as the family goes, so go the individuals of that family who will one day make up society. I'm sorry to say it, but while we are in this time of pondering and preparing for the future, we must conclude that if the state of the family signals the future of the nation, we Americans are in trouble.

> If the state of the family signals the future of the nation, we Americans are in trouble. #focusonthefuture

When we think of the family in this way, we should not be surprised that it is under such attack in our time. It is the family that shapes identity more than any other institution. It is the family that imparts values. It is the family that anchors healthy souls and the family that sets the trajectory of every individual when it comes to learning, earning, worshipping, serving, giving, and connecting with the rest of society.

Americans seem to sense this even if they don't devote themselves to it. Approximately two-thirds of Americans, some 62 percent, say their family forms the majority of their personal identity.[7] While other factors like country, religious faith, ethnic group, career, etc., are also cited, the constant answer for most Americans is one institution: the family.

It makes perfect sense, then, that there should be such a battle for the family—or against the family—in our time. Control the family, control the world. Why? Because if you control the family, you shape the individual—and everything important is made up of individuals. Mother Teresa had it right. She is quoted as saying, "If you want to change the world, go home and love your family."

I can almost hear critics objecting that I'm making too much of the family, that I'm giving it just too much importance in the broader scheme of things. Well, before I even get down to the specifics of what it means to have healthy families in our time, let me show you how the family is essential to one of the tremendous global cultural battles of our day.

THE BATTLE FOR FAMILY CULTURE

Thankfully, there is good news for us in this matter of the importance of the family. We may not be able to change national trends instantly, but the fact is we can dramatically shape the cultures of our homes, which in turn shape the course of our nation. The wonderful truth is that most of what defines a family, and thus the individuals in it, are soft factors. They are not difficult or complicated. They are simple, practical things within reach of everyone who wants to have a safe, healthy, thriving family. To put it another way, the battle for the family is fought and won with the simple, daily, personal, and often invisible parts of family life.

Let's take one of the most troubling trends we see in our national life today: the rise of pornography, particularly among children. We all know that any child with a smartphone can access pornography today. We may also know that the kind of pornography readily available today is not at the level of the pinups of generations ago. Today's easily accessible, almost real-life porn has gone to a whole different level. It is vile, it is violent, and it is psychologically defiling. Rape scenes are common. Perversions of every kind abound. It is also not uncommon to come across pornography in which a person is killed before the cameras during sex scenes. These images never leave the mind.

Tragically, children are being exposed to pornography at an increasingly earlier age. In England, a toll-free service called Childline reported that, over a three-year period, more than two thousand children called the service to say that exposure to pornography had left them tormented and afraid. "One in ten of those who received psychological help was 11 or under, and 63 percent were aged 12 to 15."[8]

Yet the most troubling part of this tragedy is that most children don't set out to find pornography. Instead, it finds them. They come across porn by accident in the home, often on an older sibling's or parent's digital devices or in the link they stumbled on when doing an online search on other topics. In short, porn invades the lives of the innocent because it is in their environment. They don't seek it. It often descends on them.

The solution is the family. Porn-free families and porn-free homes make for porn-free children. Having no porn in the house and placing porn controls on all online devices are barriers to traumatic experiences children are increasingly having ever earlier in their lives. The solution for this and a thousand other challenges is for the family to be a haven from the moral bombardment coming from culture. Our families must be incubators of the good, the pure, and the wholesome.

I'd like for you to notice a pattern here that we will confront again and again. The media speak of a social problem as though it is insurmountable. They give us the feeling that massive trends are impossible to change and that we are all about to be swept up in them to our destruction. But as we will repeatedly see in these pages, the solutions are often simple, easily accomplished, very natural acts that can keep us from being damaged by the tides of our time.

Yes, pornography is a huge problem in our culture. Yet the family can arise as a barrier against this plague. The following are helpful steps you can take to be proactive:

1. Be the first conversation that your children have about sex and pornography. Don't delay having these conversations about modesty, sexuality, and pornography due to the awkwardness, not knowing

how to talk about it, or not knowing when the right time is.

2. While using screen-accountability software for the whole family is a good first step, realize that these are only a shield and there will be situations you cannot control, such as a friend's phone or tablet. Know what each device in your house is capable of doing, and know what kind of boundaries are in place at any home your child spends time in.

3. Teach your children how consuming and dangerous pornography is and what to do when an inappropriate image or video appears or when they are shown something that makes them uncomfortable.

4. Teach your children the beauty of sexuality and God's desire for love and marriage.

5. Be prepared to respond to and discuss situations when your children might be exposed to or is wrestling with pornography. Be careful about shaming them, which often leads to secrecy and isolation around this very threatening topic.

6. Engage your kids in activities that help strengthen their personal walk and commitment to purity and holiness before the Lord. Remember, boredom is a dangerous issue for kids who have personal digital devices in their hands.

Imagine the difference these steps can make. None of them are out of reach for any of us.

THE AMAZING FAMILY DINNER

Let me delve further into this matter of simple steps that make massive differences in the lives of families. Let's talk about the glorious institution of the family dinner. This happened so naturally a generation or two ago that it would have been thought odd to mention the science of the family meal or the benefits of eating together. Yet with the intrusion of technology and the often relationally broken American family, many experts are turning our attention to the astonishing benefits that come to those who simply share a meal with other family members. COVID-19 has helped bring back mealtime for a lot of families.

The evidence for the transforming benefits of family mealtime is stunning. A 2004 study found that teens who regularly ate meals together with their families experienced fewer symptoms of depression and were less likely to use drugs.[9] The Center on Addiction has also conducted some annual studies on the importance of family meals. Their 2009 study revealed that teens who ate with their families less than three times a week were more likely to receive grades of C or lower in their schoolwork. Children who ate with their families five to seven times per week reported getting mostly As and Bs in their schoolwork.[10]

A Stanford University study revealed that children who ate with their families were less likely to eat fried foods and saturated fats, choosing fruits and vegetables instead.[11] Research confirms that children who frequently eat with their families reduce their odds of being overweight, eating unhealthy foods, and engaging in disordered eating.[12]

The list of benefits goes on. At family dinners young children learn language skills, develop patience and manners, improve their fine motor skills from using utensils, and form bonds with family members that help them when connecting with people outside the home.[13] Experts confirm all this, as well as the fact that a family of four can save around thirty-five dollars per week by simply eating at a restaurant one less time per week.[14]

A fun website is TheFamilyDinnerProject.org, which is entirely devoted to the power of regular family meals. Check this site out. The project team profiles families who are changed by starting to eat together often. They suggest recipes, topics for dinner conversation, ways to draw people in from the community, and ways to handle the challenges that sometimes arise. They also present some of the science behind the genius of the simple family meal.

Here's what you can pick up from all that they report: Children who are regularly involved in family meals learn better and perform better in school. They don't just get better grades; they enjoy learning and are happier as they do. They also have higher self-esteem, likely because they feel the security of being part of a family devoted to being together and to the well-being of each individual. In addition, kids who eat with their families often are more resilient. They are tougher, less harmed by the adversities of life, and more aware that challenges can be bested and that foes can be defeated. They also bounce back when hardship comes. This is probably because they hear other family members around the table talking about what they've experienced and how they conquered obstacles.

Now, notice the vast difference a family meal makes in the lives of family members and yet how little it requires. We aren't talking about running a marathon here. You don't need to build an addition on your house or learn some dramatic new set of skills. We are talking about doing something you already do three times a day. Just do it with family, do it regularly, and work to make the experience enjoyable, loving, and even inspiring if possible. This changes lives. And these lives in turn will transform other lives.

The Example of My Dad[15]

I don't want to leave this theme of how small things can make an incredible difference in our families and our relationships. Allow me to get even more personal than I have and tell you about something I learned from my father that has changed my life and my marriage. I think you'll see this truth of simple, loving deeds making all the difference.

My father's death really took the wind out of my sails. He was the warm center of our lives, a source of calm, of gentleness, and of wisdom. As I've shared in the past few years, the void his death left was immense, and it did not take me long to realize that I needed to get away and grieve. Given what mountains have always meant to me, I knew I needed to find a quiet space among them to be alone with my God and with my memories.

I made my way to the Peaks of Otter Lodge in the Blue Ridge Mountains. I was there to tend my sorrow and loss, but I was not there to say a final goodbye. It has always meant so much to me that my father's last words were an assurance that because of Christ, he would see me again. I shared that certainty as I do now, so any goodbye would be only temporary. Of that I was convinced as I headed off to the mountains. Still, I was in pain.

So I spent time among the soaring peaks remembering Dad. I let my mind wander back to my childhood and to all that he had meant to me then and in the days since. I wept. I wrote my father a letter. I thanked him out loud for what he had given us, to my children in particular.

It was poignant to remember that on the day my dad died, I had to go home and tell my daughter, Megan, and my son, Zach, that their Papa was gone. It is a testimony to how Dad lived that after the initial jolt of grief, we immediately began talking about heaven. We envisioned Dad caught up with Jesus. We talked about how he was with Nanny C now. We imagined the peace and the glory he beheld.

I was so moved by our reflections and my dad's imprint on my children that I made them a promise. I told them that I would do all I could to be even half the father my own dad was. I assured them that if I even came close, they would be blessed. It was a moment I will never forget.

My dad's legacy was largely spiritual. He wasn't a rich man and didn't own much in the way of material possessions. But the few material things he did pass on to my children have always been dear to me. He gave them the well-worn Bibles he used for study and preaching. Imagine how those have radiated in our family! My brother also gave Zach a 410 lever-action shotgun from Papa C.

The 410 means something special to me because every time I see it, I go back to one of my favorite memories of time spent together with my father and my son. When Zach was young, he went with me once to hunt for turkeys. We didn't hear or see a thing. After some quiet hours with no turkey in sight, we connected with Dad, and he took us to his favorite spot—the backside of the Thurston farm. When we sat down, Dad chirped a few times with his old box call, and a bird answered. We bagged it together and just laughed at what seemed like a total miracle. Zach was thrilled, and a tradition with my father was passed on to my son—one that was about family and time together more than it was about hunting.

One of the Bibles brought another surprise. As I looked through the pages, I saw notes, thoughts, coffee stains, and a picture of my mother. Written in ink around the portrait were these words: "Mid, how I have missed you. It will be a grand reunion someday soon. Love, Jim."

I can't even bring myself to think about being without my wife,

Julie. I remember asking my dad, who lived without my mother for more than ten years, how he did it. After he thought for a moment, he told me what the hardest parts were for him. He said he would reach out to touch her in the middle of the night to hold her hand, and she wasn't there. That's what left him broken and alone. He said very poignantly, "I really miss her."

I knew he did. Somehow, he was able each day to put a bridge over it all, focus on the calling God had on his life, and turn his love and heart toward his children and grandchildren, who loved him dearly. His legacy of life and love live on to this day.

A persistent heart cry I hear from those in difficult or broken relationships is "All I have ever wanted is for someone to love me." Why? Because God wired us that way. In the garden before the fall, God saw Adam alone and in need of companionship. So He gave to Adam, Eve. One who was "bone of my bones and flesh of my flesh."[16] One to come alongside and do life with him. Someone to hold, caress, cherish, serve, be tender toward, and prefer above all others.

There are two truths I believe with all my heart. They guide much of my work and my understanding of the world. First, nothing is as sweet or as meaningful as to be in love with someone who actually loves you back. I believe this with all my heart and work to help everyone have relationships of just this kind. Yet I also believe the reverse. The second truth is that little in this world is as painful and as damaging as being in a relationship with someone who is supposed to love you but doesn't.

Because of these two truths, I'm constantly urging people to consider the legacy of love they are leaving. I'm forever trying to get them to consider what prevents them from loving the people they are supposed to love as deeply as they possibly can. Are we moving too fast? Are we too devoted to our devices? Are we, in short, leaving each other behind?

The simple truth is that we are made for relationships and that in all those relationships we are called to reflect the love of God through our behavior. I'm not going too far, I trust, when I say that this is nearly the meaning of life. We are put in this world to love God and the people He gives us. We should keep this commission central to our lives and then do it with all our hearts.

Your Second Chance

I can imagine someone reading the words above and feeling condemned. You believe what I've said—that we are made for loving relationships—but this has not been the pattern of your life. You feel like a failure. You have regrets. I want you to know that you can make a turn. You can determine now that your life is going to be about the loving relationships you are meant to enjoy and to foster. I also want you to not be too hard on yourself. You may look at your life and see relationships that were tense or conflict-filled or distant. Please know that all relationships go through their challenging seasons. The question isn't whether you are going to have trouble in a given relationship. The question is what you do or don't do during those troubling seasons, which makes all the difference.

I've given these hard relational seasons a great deal of thought. Let me suggest some actions that will make a vast difference as you commit yourself to loving relationships in the future:

- Be quick to say you're sorry. Pride kills a loving relationship. Humility builds loving relationships. If you are wrong, say so. Quickly. Sincerely. Gently.

- Give yourself to the godly building blocks of relationships: prayer, worship, and gratitude. Do this with those you love, and God will draw you even more closely together.

- Focus on the good of the ones you love rather than yourself. Prefer them. Put them and their interests first. This is what love does.

- Be kind. Practice loving words and gentle ways. Always, always be generous.

- Be physical in nonsexual ways. Engage in much hand-holding, much stroking and loving touch. We are physical beings, and we often receive from loving touch even more than we do from loving words.

- Find the pleasures you enjoy together, and build on them. What are the hobbies you both love, the places, the food, the pleasures? Build on these, and have fun doing it. And by the way, laugh a lot together.

- Finally, fight fair. When tense times come, don't dig up old wrongs. Don't insult and manipulate. See an argument as an opportunity to cleanse a wound, to listen, and to explain in a way that will make you better together. If you will make your times of fighting safe and productive, you will get better each time, and the tense seasons will decrease.

If you are struggling in your relationship, you don't have to try to do everything all at once. Start with prayer and kindness. Find a pastor or Christian counselor if you need a third party to guide you. Think about your legacy.

After my dad told me that he would reach for my mom's hand in the night after she passed and she wasn't there, I realized something profound. Through the years of marriage, my parents had learned to hold hands while they slept. This small act embodies so many of the encouragements I mentioned above: kindness, nonsexual touch, intimacy, and safety.

Not long ago, I came across a beautiful story of lifelong commitment. Tom and Delma Ledbetter, a couple married for sixty-two years with two children, seven grandchildren, and seven great-grandchildren, were enjoying retirement together. Friends and family saw the couple as content and appreciating their relationship to the end. When Tom and Delma became sick and went into hospice within days of each other, their nurses set up their hospital beds next to each other. They eventually passed within an hour of each other, holding hands.[17]

Here's the lesson: in this culture where love has been degraded to a feeling, learn to hold hands while you sleep. I know it is as simple a step as having a family meal or making our homes porn-free. Yet it is steps like these that make a massive difference in our lives and those we love.

A LOVING FAMILY CULTURE

Now, let me tell you the secret of what we are talking about here. It is captured in the word *culture*. Like many people, when you think about this word, you might think of art, symphonies, ballet, and concerts. This is certainly one use of the word. We sometimes say that individuals are "cultured," meaning they are learned or experienced or sophisticated in their tastes.

However, the way I want to use the word *culture* is different. The meaning that I intend here has to do with what is encouraged to grow. To be specific, I want us to think about what the cultures of our families are. In other words, what are we encouraging to grow in our families? This compelling question will help our families to be prepared for the future.

Like me, you have probably been in a family home that had a certain feel. Perhaps you've been in the home of angry people.

They may not even have realized it, but their manner was just hostile. They dealt with each other harshly. They spoke angrily to people on TV. They told stories about how they gave that store clerk a piece of their mind. You got the feeling that they were proud of their anger. The whole atmosphere of their manner together was harsh, somewhat resentful, and, well, just raw. It was as though something terrible happened just before you walked into the room, and it left everyone furious, but you never did find out what it was.

Then, of course, I have been in genuinely loving and peaceful homes that felt like a bit of heaven to me. You could tell the people had a long, caring experience with each other. It was evident that while they may have had challenging moments with each other, they had forgiven and overcome. They spoke kindly to each other. They served each other. They showed respect and care and interest in what each had experienced.

What I'm describing in both these cases is the family culture. In the first family, the things that are encouraged to grow are grievance, bitterness, offense, and maybe even rage. This is the family culture. It taints everything they do. In the second home, the family works for a culture of love. It likely isn't easy, and it has probably been challenged, yet they work hard to build a family life in which love is encouraged to grow.

What we are learning and science is confirming is that the culture of a family can either hinder or create possibilities for everyone in the family. While I don't believe family is destiny, I do believe it leaves a strong, lifelong propensity toward the culture it fosters. We call it multigenerational flow, which is the belief that families tend to reproduce themselves. It isn't hard to imagine what the individual lives of that angry family might be. We can picture their son being an angry basketball player who gets thrown out of nearly every game and then becomes an angry husband and father. We can imagine people medicating their grievances with alcohol or drugs, food, or pleasure. We can see all their relationships dissolving over time. And, of course, we can imagine just the opposite for the loving family. Family cultures shape individual cultures, which in turn can create wonderful disasters or possibilities.

THE BATTLE TO FORGIVE

We all know from our own experience that offense and the bitterness that comes from it are some of the most significant challenges of life. Hard and wounding things happen in this life. We can't avoid them. Jesus warned us that "offenses will come."[18] What most of us struggle with is the bitterness that can come from those offenses and wounds. The poison of bitterness can dominate our lives if we aren't careful. You've likely seen people with what the book of Hebrews calls a "root of bitterness,"[19] and perhaps you've even had this same defiling force in your own life for a time.

While the battle to forgive is one that all people face, we are learning that the culture of a loving Christian family can make people more willing to forgive, more willing to extend mercy, and more willing to forget the offense. This is testimony to the power of family culture.

The research on this subject is fascinating, as seen in a 2019 Barna Group study of Christian adults. To 61 percent of married respondents, "not seeking punishment or retribution is a key element of forgiveness." Only 51 percent of never-married respondents have the same view. Similarly, 72 percent of married individuals say that forgiveness is about simply repairing relationships. A lower percentage (62 percent) of never-married individuals agree.[20] In other words, being married moves people toward a deeper willingness to forgive.

The differences between married people and unmarried people when it comes to perspectives about forgiveness are intriguing. For example, notice the distinction between single and married Christians when it comes to what forgiveness means: compared with 22 percent of married respondents, 30 percent of single respondents say forgiveness involves "restoring a relationship *without* forgetting the offense." In addition, 33 percent of single Christians can think of a person they "don't *want* to forgive," but only 24 percent of married Christians say the same thing. And 28 percent of singles, versus 21 percent of married individuals, admit there is someone they "just can't forgive."[21]

Married couples also more readily receive forgiveness. Only 19 percent of married people but 30 percent of single individuals said they had yet to accept forgiveness for a particular issue.[22]

Amazingly, a tendency toward charity and forgiveness increases when a married couple has children. The same Barna Group report captures this phenomenon well:

> When asked about a sense of charity toward various groups, practicing Christians in the child-rearing years are more likely than those who aren't to express high levels of compassion for the poor (55% vs. 48%), for criminals (13% vs. 7%) or even for people who have wronged them (18% vs. 11%).
>
> Given these compassionate attitudes, it makes sense that a pattern continues in looking at reports of giving and receiving unconditional forgiveness. Parents of children under 18 see a spike here (69% have received, 83% have offered), especially mothers (72% vs. 66% of fathers have received, 88% vs. 78% of fathers have offered).... Single fathers look more like those who don't have children in their reported experiences of unconditional forgiveness (71% have offered, 54% have received).[23]

There are a lot of statistics here, but look at the amazing conclusion. Family life highly correlates to an increased tendency toward charity and forgiveness. It makes people more willing to heal relationships and forget wrongs done to them. It also makes them better able to receive forgiveness for the wrongs they have done. All this is testimony to what a family culture has the potential to produce.

Yet let's not limit this just to the experience of the individual family. Let's allow our imaginations to roam a bit, and let's envision what might happen in a society in which healthy families are sending out generous, forgiving, kindhearted people who in turn shape that society by how they live. Imagine what this might mean. Imagine how the harsh, angry tone of American society today would change. And the tone of our politics. And the treatment of the hurting and downtrodden. And care for foreigners. Just think about what healthy families could do in our nation on just this one issue of forgiveness.

THE ONLINE WAR

Now, keep that healthy family in mind as we look at a related aspect of the family. You've seen, as I have, the incredible rise of online fighting, bullying, and even assault that is happening in our age. It's tainting our politics. It's making our social interactions far less civil. In extreme cases, students in high schools and colleges have sometimes committed suicide over online bullying and berating.

It is interesting that when surveys are conducted about who is arguing and raging online, no one seems to want to admit to it. In one survey, 21 percent of all adults said they sometimes argue online, 24 percent said they rarely do, and 55 percent said they never fight online. [24] Well, someone is doing the arguing because angry online ranters are tainting our nation!

Perhaps the most we can know with any certainty is the general trend of online arguing. Millennials argue online more than baby boomers, practicing Christians more than non-Christians, Republicans and Democrats more than Independents, and white adults more than nonwhite adults.[25] I love the phrase Dave Ramsey once tweeted to describe the hostile attitude online: "no class and digital courage."[26] We have all seen that, even among some of our Christian brothers and sisters.

Remember, we are still imagining what a healthy family can mean to a society. So it is beneficial to read the words of Roxanne Stone, editor in chief at the Barna Group, who has conducted valuable research in this arena:

> Our most fraught conversations seem to have moved from the dinner table to the screen.... However there are very few rules of etiquette in place for the internet yet. Where once family members could put a stop to an argument with a cry of "no religion or politics at the table!" the digital world does everything to encourage such debates. And, of course, it's a lot easier to be an anonymous jerk to a stranger than it is to yell at your mom.[27]

Here again, we see that healthy family cultures prevail. Where a family has meals together and discusses important topics, dialogue is fruitful, civility rules, and learning takes place. Love conditions the consideration of perspectives that may be new or even disturbing. Relationships are maintained despite differences. Yet when heated discussions move from the family dinner table to the computer screen, the natural corrections of the family aren't present, and this leads to the bombastic, insulting, unproductive behavior we often see online.

THE TRANSFORMING FAMILY

I want to illuminate an important principle here: what happens in a family gets amplified in the lives of its members. A little bit of discipline, for example, can provide the pillars for conduct that last a lifetime. When a few words, a few routines, a few traditions are established, lives are aligned for decades. The truth is that the family is an incubator. Small things grow there that later become large. Yet those little things are vital to healthy lives.

Think about your own family life for a moment. Think back on what occurred in your early home life that shaped you for a lifetime. Now, I had an exceptional set of parents, but I can remember specific sentences, specific family traditions, or individual episodes that have shaped me every day of my life. This is the God-ordained power of family. Even the smallest happenings imbed meaning, truth, love, and inspiration into the hearts of its members.

The thrilling part of this is that the things that make so much difference in a family don't necessarily spring from research and degrees and in-depth scientific investigation. Sometimes they are simply intuitive. One of my favorite stories is of a mom who changed the world through her faithful and sacrificial impact on her own home. This single mom, living in poverty, worked several jobs to make ends meet while her children were at home watching TV. She realized that the wealthy people in the places where she worked read many books and rarely watched TV. Though this mother of two boys never learned to read (unbeknownst to her children), she removed the television from their home and chose to send her children to the library to read two books a week and submit a book report to her. Even though she could not read, she would grade their papers as if she could. Her vision for her sons' future was firm and faithful. She made daily sacrifices and worked several jobs to meet her family's basic needs, all while holding on to her convictions. Her vision, sacrifice, and focus paid off. One of those little boys grew up to be a retired neurosurgeon and an American conservative political voice of reason, Dr. Ben Carson.[28]

This is why something as simple as a family meal, a hug, a kind word, a bit of discipline, or a meaningful tradition can change a life and thus change the world. We are helped by science when it comes to the family, but it doesn't take massive amounts of technical knowledge to build a family that launches healthy, loving, achieving, and godly individuals into the world.

A recent study of the characteristics of spiritually vibrant families reveals how simple and frankly enjoyable most of the habits of these households truly are. This survey concluded that three basic behaviors make for spiritually vibrant households:

- Spiritual practices like prayer and Bible study

- Spiritual conversations about God and faith

- Hospitality, or welcoming nonfamily as regular guests[29]

I love this breakdown because it puts the building blocks of spiritually healthy families within reach of every person. The truth is that everyone can pray, converse, read the Bible, and open his or her home. None of this is too complicated, and all of it is transforming.

Let's break this down further so you can see how doable these practices are. Consider these responses from people surveyed about what made their families alive spiritually:

- We play games daily—32 percent

- We have household meetings—68 percent

- We share how we're feeling with each other daily—59 percent

- We go on walks monthly—55 percent

- We go to the park monthly—48 percent

- A household member talks with me about God's forgiveness—76 percent

- A household member encourages me to go to church—71 percent

- A household member sets an example—73 percent

- A close friend visits on a regular basis—56 percent

- I have deep conversations with close friends—55 percent[30]

The above list covers the more corporate experiences of spiritually vibrant households. Consider the following responses about individual experiences:

- I personally prayed to God in the past week—80 percent

- I personally attended a religious small group or Bible study in the past week—51 percent

- I personally read from the Bible in the past week—76 percent

- I borrow household items from close friends—27 percent

- I ask close friends for help—37 percent

- We get outside help with childcare—13 percent

- I have close friends in my life who feel like family—91 percent

- I have close friends over for dinner—44 percent

- I go on vacation with close friends—32 percent

- I pray with friends who visit—58 percent[31]

I have to tell you, these responses make me realize what I already knew from my own family: spiritually alive and vibrant families are just fun and engaging. In fact, in this survey, half of the respondents "call their home life 'playful.'" A third play games together, three-quarters eat dinner together, nearly three-fifths share their feelings with each other daily, a third do housework or yard work together several times a week, and over two-thirds have regular family meetings.[32] How hard is any of this? And how much fun!

Now, let's add one more feature to the healthy, vibrant families we are imagining. Let's put these families regularly in church. Again, it's a simple step in everyone's reach. Yet consider this: 78 percent of married couples who attend church together regularly say they are "extremely happy" or "very happy" with their relationship, while just 59 percent of the couples in which only the wife attends church say they are "very happy."[33]

Here is another truly revealing statistic: praying together is the strongest predictor of relationship quality or happiness between a married couple. Couples "who report praying together frequently...are 17 percentage points more likely to say they are very happy together."[34]

I've added these last bits of information because I want you to see that while we are facing huge opposition to the family in our time, the steps toward a healthy, spiritually vibrant family are easily doable. Spend time together. Talk and eat together. Pray, read the Bible, and talk about God together. Work together.

Practice hospitality. Make sure the family regularly attends church. Anyone can do these things, and research reveals that these steps lead to happy, whole, resilient people who can withstand the moral onslaughts of our age.

Dr. Dobson sure had it right: Our challenge isn't in the specifics of how to have a thriving family. Our challenge is in deciding to "focus on the family" in the first place. Once we do, once we commit ourselves to our families and the legacies we can leave with them, the practical steps are so simple they almost happen naturally.

Thank God for Dr. Dobson. Thank God for the time we now have to ponder our future as a nation and consider what steps we ought to take to prepare ourselves. Thank God that though the family is powerful in its impact, it is simple to steer and a joy to be part of.

CHAPTER 4

THE WAR ON MEN

A s I MENTIONED earlier, not too long ago, Dr. James Dobson was given the Winston Churchill Lifetime Achievement Award by the Faith & Freedom Coalition. It happened at a sparkling gala in Washington, DC, all arranged by the coalition's founder, Ralph Reed. I had the privilege of attending this event, and I will never forget what happened there.

Two days before, President Trump had honored Dr. Dobson for his magnificent years of service on behalf of faith and the family. Affairs of state kept the president from attending the award ceremony, but he was so eager to show his support that he asked Vice President Mike Pence to acknowledge Dr. Dobson at the event.

What a glorious evening! A huge crowd was in attendance. Everyone enjoyed a delicious meal and lovely tributes from prominent speakers. The vice president gave a moving speech describing all that Dr. Dobson had accomplished and how this great man had profoundly changed the life of a young Christian named Mike Pence. It was a beautiful moment.

Then, Dr. Dobson stepped to the podium to wild applause. He was clearly overwhelmed. As the crowd hushed, Dr. Dobson surveyed the room for quite some time, adjusted the microphone, and then looked around the room some more. Finally, he leaned forward and said, "I wish my dad were here."

Now, I want you to remember that Dr. Dobson was eighty-one years old at the time. He was, as he still is, one of the most respected Christian voices in the world. He has worked with presidents, has produced media that has shaped a generation, and was being honored by a president, a vice president, and a grateful nation.

But what was on his mind? "I wish my dad were here."

THE CRY FOR THE FATHER

All of us in the room that night understood what Dr. Dobson was saying. Few things are more powerful than the bond between a father and a son. There is also nothing more profound than the imprint a good father leaves upon the life of his son. At that momentous occasion, when he was receiving one of the greatest honors of his life, eighty-one-year-old James Dobson simply wanted his dad to be there.

I remember that my mind immediately went to the story of Joseph in the Bible. You recall that after he had suffered much in his life, Joseph eventually rose to become second-in-command in all Egypt. It was then that he had the opportunity first to help his brothers and then to reveal his true identity to them—they had encountered him as a powerful Egyptian official, but they had no idea he was their brother. Remember that these brothers were the very schemers who had sold him into slavery. It was such a moving experience that Joseph wept, so loudly that the entire household of Pharaoh heard it.

And what was his first question after all this happened? "Is my father still living?" Then, soon after, he told his brothers to go back and "bring my father down here quickly."[1]

He had suffered much and risen to great heights, but in the

moment of restoration, it was his father he most wanted to have with him.

Dr. Dobson's words and the story of Joseph together almost form the cry of our generation. Where are the fathers? Where are our dads? Where are the men willing to shape the next generation?

I can tell you as a dad myself that we fathers feel the reverse of this cry of the sons. I find it striking when I read Paul's appeal to Timothy, his son in the faith, in the last chapter of the final letter the great apostle ever wrote. Paul is in prison, and you can tell from what he writes that he knows he is about to die. So what does he want Timothy to do for him in the last days of his life? "Do your best to come to me quickly. ... When you come, bring the cloak that I left with Carpus at Troas, and my scrolls, especially the parchments."[2]

I love this. "Get to me. Hurry. And bring my coat, my books, and my magazines. I need you now."

It strikes me as I recall these stories that God has intended the connection between generations to be so powerful that to live without it results in destruction. We learn this from the very last verse in the Old Testament. The prophet Malachi tells us that the Lord desires to "turn the hearts of the parents to their children, and the hearts of the children to their parents." But if it does not happen, God will "come and strike the land with total destruction."[3]

> A fatherless America is at the heart of the men's crisis and a hundred other dysfunctions society suffers from today because men, for the most part, are not what they should be.
> #focusonthefuture

I'm sorry to say it so harshly, but this is the condition of most of America today. We have a generational disconnect, particularly between fathers and sons. In fact, let me go further. A fatherless America is at the heart of the men's crisis and a hundred other dysfunctions society suffers from today because men, for the most part, are not what they should be.

WHAT THE FUTURE CAN BE

Now, having stated this so negatively, I want also to state my firm belief that the situation we face with men in our generation is fixable. We really can turn this around. Why do I believe this? I believe it because God is real and powerful, and He is reaching to men today. I believe it because men are miserable living as our secular society has urged them to live, and they are hungry for something more. I also believe it because whenever I see a crisis in our society, I know it is an opportunity for biblical truth to prevail. Finally, I believe it because the reality is that we have not been in this downward spiral of manhood for long. This means we truly can turn things around.

I believe this last point because I remember what manhood was like when I was a boy. I grew up at a time when what has come to be known as the Greatest Generation led our nation. I remember the pride. I remember the love of country. I remember how valiant men fought fierce enemies abroad and then came home, put up their uniforms, and used that same character, courage, and skill to lift our nation to new heights. That generation shaped me, and I will never stop thanking God for it.

Not long ago, someone sent a photo to me of the USS *Pennsylvania* as it was during World War II. She was one of the super-dreadnaught battleships in the US Navy of those days, and she was a beauty. Receiving that photo was a tender moment for me because a plaque dedicated to that heroic ship hung on the wall of our family home all the time I was growing up. As

I mentioned earlier, my father served on that ship. It was a harrowing experience for him. He raised me on stories of kamikaze planes and torpedoes hitting the hull and of the death and horror all wars create. When Dad came home, he disembarked his ship, kissed the ground, and went about serving his God with even greater devotion than he had served his nation.

We kids got enormous doses of World War II lore in our early days just as we got large doses of our noble family history in the military. My great-grandfather served in the American Civil War as a boy. The story is that Abraham Lincoln himself walked up to my towheaded ancestor and said, "Son, you are a mighty young lad to be serving in the military." That military heritage continues in my family to this day. My older brother went into the Marine Corps. My older sister's husband served in the army. My other sister's husband served in Vietnam and was awarded the Purple Heart, and my youngest sister's husband served in the army. Still another of my sisters' husbands served in the navy, I served in the US Army Reserve, and my younger brother served in the National Guard.

We were all obviously shaped by the martial history of our clan, yet I can tell you that what stuck with me most was the imprint of the Greatest Generation's brand of masculinity. Dad told us about the sacrifices of the men he had known in war. He took us to the nearby DuBois, Pennsylvania, cemetery and tenderly spoke of how freedom isn't free and how we can worship God openly only because other people fought and died for us. As I've said, my father flew the American flag in our yard every day, and that flag came to symbolize all the heritage, sacrifices, values, and devotion that my father spoke so powerfully about as I was growing up.

I think of Dad every time I hear the Toby Keith song "Courtesy of the Red, White, and Blue." One line in particular touches me—when it mentions his dad flying the flag in their yard until the day he died—because this was my father.

All that valor, all those inspiring stories, seemed to live in my father and make him the man of sterling character I loved so much. Dad taught us from the well that was within him. He told us boys that a man cherishes a woman and honors her for who she is. My father never yelled at my mother, not once, though I can tell you that my mother was a strong woman who might have angered a lesser man. Dad treated Mom like a lady. He did it naturally and in an unforced way. He also did it while constantly explaining to me that this is what a man did. Real men were measured, in part, by how they protected, served, and devoted themselves to the women in their lives. I've never forgotten such lessons of manhood from my father's lips and life.

In fact, it was a conflict between my understanding of masculinity and Dad's sterling character that created one of my earliest crises about how a man ought to behave. You see, my father, as I've said, was the kindest man I ever met. He was a gentle soul who was quicker to turn the other cheek than he was to fight back. I loved him for it, but as I got older, I started to resent the fact that he sometimes wouldn't stand up for himself. People took him for granted and used his gentle personality and loving ways for their own advantage. I wanted him to push back. I remember getting angry that he would take the high road when I thought he should be calling people out for their vicious ways. I wanted him to stand up for what I thought was right, even if it meant, as I would have said at the time, "knocking some heads."

I remember that one episode, in particular, was uniquely painful. We grew up in a fairly rural setting, and this sometimes meant that the people we were around could be very strict about matters of religion. Our family was strict about biblical matters, but we resisted the temptation to add our own rules to the standards of God. We wanted to please God, but we didn't want to lay legalistic burdens on people.

Not everyone felt this way, and they had no reservations about expressing their views in deeply hurtful ways. Though my parents set high moral standards for us children, they did allow my sisters to wear makeup, something that was a bit controversial among some of the Christians we knew. I suppose my parents expected everyone to live and let live. Instead, the people who disagreed with my parents started hurling insults. I remember my father, a devoted pastor and servant of God, being deeply wounded when some of the people he served started calling him a hypocrite. I couldn't believe it and hoped my father would fire back; he never did. He loved. He prayed. He kept serving the same people who accused him of letting his daughters follow the ways of the world.

Though I chafed at my dad's lack of fighting instinct, I learned from him. I learned the power of the soft answer turning away wrath. I learned that the godly man answers first with prayer in all matters. I learned the power of humility and that true masculinity isn't about an ability to dominate or seek revenge but rather an ability to exercise self-control in all things. This was the imprint my father and the majority of the Greatest Generation left on their sons and daughters.

OPEN SEASON ON MEN

Sadly, we are not living today in the times in which I grew up. Things are quite different, and I'm sorry to say that there is a war on men and righteous manhood in our nation today. Rather than seeing men and women as partners in divine destiny, bound in mutual encouragement for the good of both, many want a war of the sexes, banishing one gender in favor of the other. It will not work. It is not wise. It will not produce God's best and highest. It is yet another form of oppression that comes from wrong ideas and oppressive leftist politics.

Unquestionably, men have been irresponsible, and this is at the root of what we see in society. I admit this openly as I will again and again in this chapter. Yet I want you to understand that most of the irresponsibility of younger men is a result of deep dysfunctions absorbed from our dysfunctional society. Our men's crisis has resulted from a convergence of some of the most deep-seated ills of American life today.

It begins, certainly, with the high divorce rates among baby boomers, which is the fruit of the sexual revolution of decades ago. When sex was made legitimate outside marriage, when people married—if they ever did—for personal pleasure and fulfillment rather than a biblical covenant and commitment to the next generation, and when men and women abandoned biblical responsibilities, divorce became a scourge in our nation.

This is agonizing to everyone involved—men, women, and children. Yet research has long confirmed that it is young men who absorb the impact of divorce most deeply, most torturously.[4] Not only are they more deeply wounded by divorce than perhaps their sisters are, but then these boys are usually left to grow up in homes led by women and often women who are angry with the men in their lives—their boys' fathers in particular.

As a result, in these situations, there is no one in the home to model manhood. There is no one to help a young boy know who he is as a man. There is no one to call out noble manhood from his young soul. Young men want to belong. They want to test themselves. They want to know if they have what it takes. Many of them want to fulfill King David's charge to his son Solomon: "Be strong, ...and show yourself a man."[5] But most boys don't have anyone to guide them in this.

I want to pause here to say that I am taking nothing away from the heroic single mothers in our world by saying this. Thank God for the moms who have done the best job they can do with their sons. Many of these mothers were forced into single parenthood by circumstances far beyond their control, often by irresponsible men. They stepped up. They spoke to their sons about what it means to be a man. They challenged and prayed and involved other men and sacrificed in the hope that their sons would be great men.

I respect these mothers. I love them and honor their devotion. Yet I mean no insult when I say that it just isn't possible for a woman to be a "daddy/mom." And no one should be asked to be both parents.

So, our plague of divorce has taken men from homes—or they have sinfully fled the house—thus leaving boys to figure out manhood on their own. They can't. No one can. And our nation suffers from a dearth of good men on the rise.

Then there is the crisis of manhood created by the feminist movement. Before anyone draws the wrong conclusions, let me say loudly and firmly that I am devoted to honoring women. I believe that what has befallen women throughout history at the hands of abusive, neglectful, arrogant, misguided men has been a travesty. It is no wonder women began to push back. It is no wonder that they refused to accept what irresponsible and vile men visited upon them. The version of the feminist movement that was a legitimate pushback against evil and that righted wrongs that made the heavens weep was a good thing, and good men should support it. Thank God for much of what women are accomplishing today.

> The version of the feminist movement that was a legitimate pushback against evil and that righted wrongs that made the heavens weep was a good thing, and good men should support it. #focusonthefuture

However, we also have to realize that there is a version of the feminist movement that is simply anti-man. While it may have initially focused on addressing legitimate wrongs and inequalities, it went much further than that. It evolved into hatred. It concocted a philosophy of men being inferior beings and being incapable of living successfully in the modern world.

Men were needed during the settlement of the nation when someone had to build the cities, lay the steel, and fight off enemies. Yet now that the more muscular phase of our national development is done, according to this extreme version of feminism, it falls to the women to lead because men do not possess the intelligence and the sensibilities to live effectively in the information age of today. Women must rise. Men do not fit. They are not to be trusted. In fact, they may have to be restrained. This is what the darker, more hate-filled side of the feminist movement maintains. And it is harming men—boys in particular—and thus harming our nation and our future.

Then, combine the devastations of our divorce rates and the dark side of the feminist movement with the snowballing impact of the radical LGBTQ movement. I don't think I'm paranoid when I say that this movement is intently anti-man, entirely against any vision of righteous masculinity. It emphasizes the feminine. It sees manhood not as a gift and calling from God, as a mandate for virtue and service, but rather as a curse. This movement believes that since all gender is a choice by humans and not by God, most men have poorly chosen. They have given in to aggression and domination because they have not "evolved," have not been "enlightened."

Unfortunately, this view has taken up residence in many of our universities. Courses and programs on "toxic masculinity" are increasing.[6] Traditional manhood—let me call at least some of it biblical manhood—is treated as a plague on society. Professors blame everything from war and abuse to disease and ignorance on the dominance of males throughout much of history.

Just consider some of the popular books that describe this disturbing trend. Keep in mind that these are serious books by serious authors released by serious publishers. You may know the name Philip Zimbardo. He was the architect of the famous Stanford prison experiment of 1971. He published a book based on a popular TED talk he had given. The name? *The Demise of Guys: Why Boys Are Struggling and What We Can Do About It.* Now, this book was an attempt to champion well-intentioned manhood and its impact on boys. Still, this eminent scholar noted a trend: the demise of guys.

The prominent writer Hanna Rosin penned a book entitled *The End of Men: And the Rise of Women.* Kay Hymowitz wrote *Manning Up: How the Rise of Women Has Turned Men Into Boys.* And the notable sociologist Roy Baumeister gave us a book entitled *Is There Anything Good About Men? How Cultures Flourish by Exploiting Men.* Not all these authors are anti-man, but all see the same trends toward disdain and disregard for masculinity. I could name dozens of other similar books. I could also describe university courses that portray manhood as a plague and an enemy of civilization. Yet you get the point. "Men bad—very bad. Men dangerous—very dangerous. Must stop men."

Of course, the political Left champions all this with a goose-stepping ferocity that rips our nation apart. I wish I could be kinder, but I cannot. The truth is that the political Left in America has become a mirror image of what it claims to abhor. It has become a form of terrorism, seeking to either dominate its opposition or destroy it.

The American political Left will drive a man out of business rather than allow him to make moral decisions about what kind of business he will conduct. The American political Left will sue and threaten to destroy one of the nation's most popular and prosperous companies all because that company is owned by people who do not wish to pay for abortions. The American political Left will try to bully Catholic hospitals into performing abortions rather than respect religious principles that have shaped that church for centuries.

I think just a few words from Hillary Clinton show us what the American political Left has become. In 2015, then–Secretary of State Hillary Clinton told a global conference of women in New York that when it comes to abortion, "deep-seated cultural codes, religious beliefs and structural biases have to be changed."[7] Imagine the stridency of this. To accommodate the abortionist aspirations of the American political Left, religious Americans will simply have to change what they believe, the tenets of their ancient faiths. Stunning, really!

Yet this is also the tone of the approach that the American political Left takes toward men. In championing policies that encourage divorce, in supporting the most extreme elements of feminism and the radical LGBTQ movement, the Left has also become stridently anti-man. There is a conspiratorial effort to shame and silence men, to cut them out of the fabric of American cultural life, and to remove their voice.

I'm familiar with this dynamic because I spend a great deal of time working with the mentally ill and see a similar trend. In American society there has inadvertently been a systemic mistreatment of the mentally ill. They have been stigmatized, shamed, and silenced. To correct this, specific strategies have been designed to restore the voice of the mentally ill, thus removing the stigmas and shame that society places on them.

This is very similar to the attitudes that have been aimed at men. They are being stigmatized mostly by the collection of misguided agendas championed by our country's political Left. The eminent Canadian clinical psychologist Jordan Peterson has exposed these efforts beautifully, and I strongly suggest you catch his interviews and speeches on YouTube, read his books, and hear him live whenever you can. He contends, as I do, that men today are being treated with the same disregard the mentally ill have been. First, they are stigmatized: *Men are toxic.* Then they are shamed: *Men are dangerous and are destroying our civilization.* Then they are silenced: *Men have held the stage for too long. Let them be silent while women take the lead.*

THE DISEASE OF MASCULINITY?

You might think I'm going too far when I say such things. Surely it isn't that bad. Well, let me lay out the evidence for you, not to discourage you but to enlist you in the great battle of our generation for powerful, righteous, principled, noble manhood. This is what we are facing in the future, and I want you to be prepared to help recover what we have lost.

Are you aware that not long ago, the American Psychological Association (APA) issued new guidelines that detail how traditional masculinity harms men and boys? The APA says it took thirteen years to develop these guidelines and that they rely on forty years of research. Yet their stunning conclusion is that "traditional masculinity is psychologically harmful." They say that in their studies "the more men conformed to masculine norms, the more likely they were to consider as normal risky health behaviors such as heavy drinking, using tobacco and avoiding vegetables, and to engage in these risky behaviors themselves."[8]

Oh my! Masculine men won't eat vegetables? Western culture is in danger, certainly!

There's more. The APA isn't sure that such a thing as pure manhood exists. One of their psychologists asks, "What is gender in the 2010s?" The answer? "It's no longer just this male-female binary."[9] Now, this is psychological jargon for saying that there is no such thing as male and female, just degrees of both in every human being.

It's no wonder that Rod Dreher responded, "I suspect this is mostly about psychologizing the gelding of American males.... The more I think about it, the more Soviet this seems. Dissent from gender ideology (not just the transgender stuff, but the establishment's view of what men and women are)? Well, [experts say] you must be insane."[10]

Yet it wasn't just Christians who were outraged by the APA's pronouncements. Professor Geoffrey Miller of the University of New Mexico, who describes himself as an agnostic, tweeted, "The American Psychological Association is using its army of clinical psychologists to wage a pseudo-therapeutic war against 'traditional masculinity,' 'patriarchy,' 'male stoicism,' and 'rigid gender norms.'"[11]

Dr. Miller is right, and nothing confirms it like the words of the APA's document itself. Consider this: "Research suggests that socialization practices that teach boys from an early age to be self-reliant, strong, and to minimize and manage their own problems on their own yield adult men who are less willing to seek mental health treatment."[12] This is more psychologist doublespeak. In other words, strong men don't turn to psychologists and therapists as much as some psychologists and therapists wish they would.

The APA standards, purporting to advise the entire universe of counseling and therapy, are nothing but an ideological attack on men typical of what is taking place in our generation. No one maintains this more than the renowned Jordan Peterson, himself a psychologist at the University of Toronto. Here is his conclusion:

> The document produced by the APA ... is disingenuous, scientifically fraudulent and ethically reprehensible. I believe that the people who wrote it are ill-informed,

ideologically possessed, morally weak, and malevolent in their unacknowledged and overweening resentment. I am embarrassed and ashamed to have them speak on behalf of my profession, and would like to apologize to the public for not having been sufficiently awake and out-raged earlier to have done more to stop something like this from happening.[13]

Yet Peterson and other psychologists who dissent from the APA's war on manhood do wish that the organization would focus itself on the forces that are threatening to destroy healthy masculinity today. Among the most damaging of these is a lack of fathers in the home. Here is where the real battleground is, and—prepare yourself!—just how devastating this trend is will likely shock you.

THE PLAGUE OF FATHERLESSNESS

The horrible truth is that some 23 percent of children in America live in single-parent homes—"the world's highest rate."[14] Some folks I've met simply throw up their hands when they hear this statistic and suggest that maybe single parenthood is just a new way of doing family, something like the modern trends toward cohabiting or same-sex marriage.

Well, let me tell you that people who are tempted to believe such things are simply ill informed. The truth is that single-parent homes nearly always mean fatherless homes, and this is a horrible plague on our society. We don't need to look any fur-ther for confirmation of this than the stories of domestic terror-ists or instigators of mass shootings we've seen in the news of late. These are so stark that I'm hoping they will help to wake up America to the devastations of fatherlessness.

Just consider the pattern here. Nikolas Cruz killed fourteen students and three staff members at Marjory Stoneman Douglas

High School in Parkland, Florida, in 2018. His adoptive father died when Cruz was five, and he never knew another male role model in later years.[15]

In Charleston, South Carolina, white supremacist Dylann Roof shot nine African Americans in a church just after those church members had graciously welcomed him to their prayer meeting. His parents had been divorced before he was born, reconciled for a few years, and then divorced again when Roof was five. While he sometimes lived with his father and stepmother, his dad was away on business up to four days a week, leaving Roof's stepmother to raise him during those periods.[16]

Then perhaps you remember the name Adam Lanza. He is the young man who killed his mother and then twenty elementary school children and six staff members at Sandy Hook Elementary School in Newtown, Connecticut. Adam had not talked to his father in the two years prior to that traumatic incident.[17]

And so it goes. I've said that fatherlessness is a plague on America. Perhaps you see why. Then consider this: 75 percent of adolescent murderers are from fatherless homes. Some "63 percent of youth suicides are from fatherless homes," and "85 percent of children with behavioral disorders have only a mother in the home."[18] I'll say it again: fatherlessness is a plague on our land.

Let me continue to let the facts speak for themselves:

- 85 percent of all children with behavioral disorders come from fatherless homes.

- 90 percent of all homeless and runaway children come from fatherless homes.

- 71 percent of all high school dropouts are from fatherless homes.

- 75 percent of all teens in treatment for chemical abuse are from fatherless homes.

- 80 percent of rapists motivated by misplaced anger come from fatherless homes.

- 70 percent of juveniles in state institutions are from fatherless homes.

- 85 percent of all youths in prisons are from fatherless homes.[19]

I could go on, but let's just cut to the chase and put these statistics in raw terms. Children from fatherless homes are five times more likely to commit suicide, thirty-two times more likely to run away, twenty times more likely to have behavioral disorders, fourteen times more likely to commit rape based on anger, nine times more likely to end up in a state institution of some kind, and twenty times more likely to end up in prison than children with a father in the home.[20]

Then consider the devastation of fatherless homes to young women. Daughters from single-parent, fatherless households "are 53 percent more likely to marry as teenagers, 711 percent more likely to have children as teenagers, 164 percent more likely to have a pre-marital birth and 92 percent more likely to get divorced themselves."[21]

BOYS AND PORNOGRAPHY

You see, then, why I call fatherlessness a plague upon our land. The facts are stunning, aren't they? But let me show you how crisis builds on crisis in this area for men and boys. Let me explore with you how, in an era in which nearly a quarter of American homes are without a father, another plague is able to devastate our young men. This plague is the massive challenge of young men and pornography.

In fact, this challenge is so huge that I don't want to refer to it as a plague. I want to refer to it as a tsunami. You see, a tsunami is a different phenomenon from the natural forces that create waves in the seas. Most waves are generated by the gravitational pull of the sun and the moon. We can see it on the surface and usually know what to expect.

A tsunami, though, begins with an event, one that usually starts under the surface of the water. A subsurface earthquake can create it. There is a hidden disruption, and by the time you can see the full power of what has been released, it is often too late. Warnings won't help. Everything in the path of the tsunami is suddenly and violently swept away. Such horrors fill our news headlines when they occur.[22]

This is the power of the cultural force that is traumatizing us today. As with a natural tsunami, it all started with a slight disruption. This disruption sent out shock waves that remained largely under the surface of our times, mostly undetected. In recent decades, the force has gained speed and power. Now, it is making itself known and at such a stunning pace that our cultural warning systems may not serve us well. What I'm talking about is the cultural tsunami of internet pornography.

Here is the really horrible news. While this tsunami of filth is permeating our whole society, it is severely impacting one group in particular: teenage boys. This may come as a surprise. Perhaps we envisioned older men as the ones most drawn to internet pornography. Perhaps we thought it might be men in their twenties or thirties who would most be tangled up in this dark web. It isn't true. The most recent statistics tell us that 93 percent of teen boys (and 62 percent of teen girls) have seen online porn by the age of 18.[23] And the added tragedy is that it is just this age group that is weakened and made susceptible by an absence of fathers.

It gets worse. In our time, young boys nearly always own or have access to cell phones or tablets that allow them to access pornography if they choose. Now, don't picture pinups from the

World War II era or even the usual fare of magazines like *Playboy*. These alone have done considerable damage. No, the kind of pornography available to boys today is the kind that portrays abuse, victims of sex trafficking, children, and graphically deviant behaviors of every kind. Add to all this the disturbing fact that boys tend to see their first pornographic image nowadays when they are just kids. Some have reported being exposed at only five years old.[24] Five years old. Think about that. The estimated national average of boys' first exposure to porn ranges anywhere from eight[25] to twelve years old.[26]

The harsh truth is that virtual reality has put live sexual chaos at the fingertips of hormone-driven, red-blooded, extremely inquisitive prepubescent and pubescent kids. Our boys are being bombarded daily by the crass and, at times, gross sexualization and objectification of women everywhere they turn. Sadly, this visual trauma takes place all through their formative years when they are setting the groundwork for what kind of men they will one day grow up to be.

American society is largely sleeping through the tsunami that is tormenting boys today. Thankfully, the #MeToo moment in our world is causing more discerning souls to realize what pornography is producing. It is a breeding ground for abuse, intimidation, and harassment. We are finally realizing that our *Playboy*, "gone wild," sex-and-titillation culture does not serve women well. This culture is actually much of the reason that such a high percentage of women report being abused.

Think about how prevalent pornography is in our society. It is as close as the nearest cell phone or iPad. It is lurking in our churches and our schools. It has even infiltrated the bedroom. I'll never forget the dire warning that we heard not long ago from evangelist and best-selling author Josh McDowell. He stated that pornography has now become "a gigantic challenge" for Christian homes and churches—and it is only getting worse.[27]

I must tell you that I feel great compassion for boys. We expect so much from them. We insist that they almost automatically grow into men with immense respect and honor for women. We imagine this happening as effortlessly as the biological changes that bring a boy into manhood. Yet we teach them little of how a man ought to conduct himself when it comes to women. We do not train them to defend the rights of women. We do not help them understand their own feelings and needs and then channel those forces into healthy, productive lanes. We also do not tend to have early and meaningful talks with them about pornography. So we expect them to know how to live counter to what society screams at them every day and all without the coaching, understanding, and compassion that ought to be theirs.[28]

One of the parts of this crisis that disturbs me most is how few fathers talk to their sons about sex and pornography. I've come to the conclusion that many of these men are wrestling with their own shame and so are clumsy and unsure about speaking to their sons. This leads me to another observation: When was the last time you heard a sermon from your church pulpit about the pornography that pervades our generation? Could it be that perhaps guilt and shame work against it? I'm not accusing. I'm trying to draw us out into the light. I have to ask why we are so reticent to address this crisis.

Some years ago, we read headlines about the Lost Boys of Sudan, the young refugees who faced tremendous loss and danger as they fled that war-torn land.[29] Now, it seems we can talk about the Lost Boys of America, the young men who are swirling in the tsunami of pornography that is robbing them of confidence, of morality, and even of righteous manhood.

THE SOCIAL MEDIA BOMBARDMENT

I pondered this recently as I looked out the window of my house on a snowy day. I could see one of the best sledding hills in our neighborhood, and I could see that it was covered by a foot of untouched snow. It wasn't long ago when that hill on such a day would have been packed with sleds. Boys would have been out there, running up and down, competing with each other with great shouting and laughter. It would have lasted for hours before exhausted boys trundled home for hot chocolate and something tasty from their mothers' kitchens.[30]

Yet that day, I saw not a soul on that perfect sledding hill. Not a single boy was out there for the thrill and the challenge. Not a shout of delight arose from that snowy wonderland. Childhood used to revolve around outdoor fun, adventure, and friendships, with caring adults at home, the church, and our communities as anchors. Today's boys, though, are rudderless. Their world is social media driven.

Here are some of the hard truths we need to know:

- Tragically, fully half of all American teens admit they feel uncontrollably addicted to their mobile devices.[31]

- The average American teenager is subjected to 14,000 sexual references and innuendos on television alone.[32]

- Of ten- to seventeen-year-old internet users, 42 percent reported seeing online pornography. Equally disturbing is that two-thirds of these stumbled onto such sites accidentally.[33]

- Some 72 percent of teenagers and young adults say TV and other media have taught them "some" or "a lot" about sex.[34]

- In a Safe America Foundation survey, 53 percent of teenagers reported landing on violent, hate-based, or pornographic websites. Of those, "91% unintentionally found the offensive sites while searching the Web."[35]

I've been talking a great deal about boys here. I don't want to be misunderstood, though, so let me state it clearly: we want to be champions for both our girls and our boys. I'm not sorry that so many academic programs promote girls today. I love the STEAM programs designed to encourage girls in science, technology, engineering, art, and mathematics. I hope these programs get even more funding and that programs designed to teach young girls leadership and empowerment continue to thrive.[36]

None of this should be diminished by my call for realizing what is happening to boys today. Our girls are flourishing for the most part, and we should celebrate this and do all we can to help them achieve. Yet we live in a society that condemns masculinity, that tells boys from an early age that they are toxic, destructive, and deformed. We have to stand with our boys and insist that masculinity is not the enemy; sin is the enemy. Our goal should be to raise young men to live out the words of Paul: "Be watchful, stand firm in the faith, act like men, be strong."[37]

The good news here is that, as I said in chapter 3, the solutions are easy to put into practice but very high impact. Everyone reading these words can mentor and encourage a young man. Everyone can spend some time with a boy, explain godly masculinity to him, inoculate him against the philosophies of this world, and impart to him a sense of nobility and value.

If you have a son, it takes very little to spend some extra time with him or go on a long drive or get out in nature and awaken the manly forces in his soul. It also takes very little to tell him how much you love him, to tell him of your hopes for him, and to speak powerful words into his life that shape him all his days. He's more than just a boy in your home, just another responsibility. He's meant to help lead his generation of men into healthy, powerful, transforming masculinity—and you are meant to help set him on this path.

Let me end this section with some firm words for fathers. Virtually every man I have ever met struggles to believe God loves him. I know this negative belief system often starts with what he sees or doesn't see, especially in his dad. We have work to do. Our boys are increasingly conflicted, confused, and broken. The good news is that it is never too late to be a good dad or mom and to exercise the influence to guide their steps from being boys to becoming men. It's up to us to point them to God—the only One who can help strengthen them or put them back together.

Let's rally, men! Let's rise and do what we are called to do. We can rescue our boys from the trends of our day if we invest and reverse the course of fatherlessness in our time. God bless you as you give this your all. The next generation is worth it.

MEN MATTER!

Now, in spite of the fact that we've just taken a good look at the challenges created by absentee fathers and declining manhood, I have no intention of defining all men by the struggles of some, diminishing the impact of godly men, or pretending men are a lost cause.

The good news, according to Pew Research, is that American fatherhood is changing. They say that even though more kids are growing up without Dad in the home, in cases where fathers do live with their kids, they are taking on a more active role than in past years. Their key findings reveal that "more dads are staying home to care for their kids" (17 percent of stay-at-home parents are dads as of 2016); more dads (57 percent) see parenting as "extremely important to their identity"; and dads are devoting more time to child care than they were fifty years ago, with fathers reporting they spent "an average of eight hours a week on child care" in 2016—triple the amount of time reported in 1965.[38] Add to this the 90 percent of Americans who agree that a father's influence is so unique that the contribution cannot be denied.[39] Again, Americans see that men matter. Americans recognize that fathers matter. Clearly, Americans do not believe the insulting labels that secular thought leaders today lay on men.

There's more. According to a recent CareerBuilder survey conducted online by The Harris Poll, the majority of today's working dads are no longer willing to take a pay cut to spend more time with their kids. Instead, they are looking for ways to bring balance to family and work, seeking to find success in both arenas. More than a third acknowledge that working causes them to miss significant events in their children's lives and nearly a quarter of them say their children have asked them to work less.[40] Imagine. In an age when we criticize men for being poor dads, they are seeking ways to spend more time with their kids as they juggle their careers. God bless them! When I talk to men and ask them how they're doing as dads, most of them say, "I think about it every day." This doesn't fit the picture of the neglectful fathers placed on most men, does it?

Dads have tremendous influence in the family. Let me remind you of Paul's words of admonition to men: "Fathers, provoke not your children to wrath: but bring them up in the nurture and admonition of the Lord."[41] Why did Paul find it necessary to say this? Because a man has this power. Because a man is hugely influential in the lives of his children, and that power can be used for good or for driving them to anger.

We've known for years now that when dads are absent, children are much more likely to experience academic problems, teen pregnancy, drug and alcohol addiction, mental health challenges, incarceration, and poverty. But when fathers are involved in their children's lives, the children are more likely to stay in school and get higher grades.[42] Even in high-crime neighborhoods, 90 percent of children who live in stable homes with a mother and father present do not drop out of school and become delinquents.[43]

They are also far less likely to become sexually active during adolescence. Meg Meeker noted in her book *Strong Fathers, Strong Daughters* that "76 percent of teen girls said that fathers influenced their decisions [for good or bad] on whether they should become sexually active."[44]

These statistics are about fatherhood, but they are also about manhood. If we are going to turn these realities around, we need more champions of men and of godly manhood—champions who will follow in the footsteps of Dr. Dobson. His research has shown that dads have a stunningly important role in their sons' lives. Their boys learn empathy from them. Boys also learn how to manage their testosterone from their dads. Thank God for this! Engaged dads guide their boys, keep them from dangerous excess, and narrate the path to healthy manhood.

This irreplaceable influence of dads applies to spiritual matters as well. When a father attends church, says Promise Keepers, there's a 93 percent chance that all others in the home will as well.[45] You did not read that wrong—93 percent! Let that sink in for a moment.

To underscore this point, when you take fathers out of the equation, the figure plummets. If Dad does *not* attend church, even if Mom is a regular attender, only one child in sixty-seven will grow up to attend church regularly. If a father is an irregular attender and mom is a regular attender, one in twenty-nine children will be regular churchgoers as adults. But if both Mom and Dad are regular attenders, one in three children will grow up to be regular church attenders.[46]

That is the power and influence of men on those who love them, and we've all seen it. Often, if a dad uses foul or obscene language, the boy he raises will do the same. If dad is angry and hateful, it's likely his son will be too. If Dad bullies people and erupts with violent outbursts, many times, so will his boy. The good news is that, conversely, if a father loves, the son learns to love also. And if dad prays, it's very likely that his son will too.

I am encouraged, and I want you to be encouraged too. Men are getting the message. Now more than ever I see a significant surge of righteous men arising to use their influence to shape the next generation for God.

I'm proud of them not only because of what they will mean in the lives of their children but also because I believe what Dr. James Dobson has taught us: "Nations that are populated largely by immature, immoral, weak-willed, cowardly, violent, and self-indulgent men cannot and will not long endure."[47] I want to continue to encourage godly men to rise up, get involved, and make a difference. The future of America depends on it. The darker the times, the more urgently God calls men to stand secure in who they are in Him and lead our families, our communities, and our nation forward.

CHAPTER 5

THE HEALING OF THE SOUL

I MAGINE A SCENE with me. You are Adam, the first man, and you live in a lush and beautiful world. Magnificent rivers are pouring down from soaring mountains. These rivers water green and vibrant land—your land, your garden. Stunningly majestic animals move about this land. They mean you no harm. They are there to serve you and for you to admire. Daily you walk in this splendid setting with God. You commune openly, face to face, without shame or shadow.

Could life be any better?

Then, one day, God seems concerned about you. Something is amiss, He says. There must be a change. You can think of nothing you need, nothing that is lacking. What must it be?

Finally, God explains: "It is not good for the man to be alone."[1]

You ponder this. You have a perfect body, you live in an idyllic setting, and you enjoy an unfettered relationship with God. You would seem to have everything you need. Yet God knows best, and He has said that you are not as you should be until you have relationships with other human beings.

"It is not good for the man to be alone."

It is a truth that sounds from the pages of Scripture and the whole of human history. We are made for relationships. We are created to love. We are made to live in community, families, and friendships—together in freedom, safety, and the presence of God.

This leads to some of the greatest certainties of life. As I mentioned in chapter 3, nothing is more beautiful than being in a relationship with someone who is supposed to love you and actually does. This is the meaning of life. This is the highest form of life we humans can know. The second is that nothing is more painful than being in a relationship with someone who is supposed to love you and doesn't. This is agony. It's a perversion of all that God intended.

Millions of people in our world today live in this kind of brokenness. All are wounded and some are abused by the very people who are supposed to love them. They are harmed, within and without, by those responsible for protecting them and caring for them.

Millions more live in isolation. Some are addicted to technology; others are so harmed that they withdraw, distance themselves, or simply don't know how to have meaningful relationships. So they live alone, apart, and without the love they were made for—a desperado complex.

Hear me. Life can be better. They can have relationships, and love can fill their lives. They can have the community, family, and friendships they were made for. We all can.

A NEW DAY DAWNS

I am sure of this because I believe God loves us and is reaching to each one of us. The Scriptures tell us that He sees the lonely in families, and I believe God is ever trying to connect us to each other. But I am also saying this because I've learned some of the exciting breakthroughs in science that confirm what God told us from the very beginning of time: "It is not good for the man to be alone."

The fact is that we've made fantastic progress in the study of the human brain in recent decades. We have mapped the brain. We can watch it work through the marvel of digital imaging. We can even track its processes and emotional responses in great detail. This helps us to know better what is healthy, promotes growth, and makes for a fulfilling life at the core of who we are.

The scientific community is in a stir about the discoveries in this fascinating field. As early as 2005, *Time* magazine declared, "Get ready for an Era of the Brain. New scanning techniques are making it easier to determine how our minds work."[2] The people at *Time* were right. A new era has dawned, and it is all the gift of what many scientists call the field of interpersonal neurobiology and others call interpersonal neuroscience.

Allan Schore, a neuroscientist at the UCLA David Geffen School of Medicine, has said, "Neuroimaging is more than finding the next drug for anxiety." Beyond this, "we can study empathy, trust, deception, emotional communication, regulation of violence—issues that are central to human existence."[3] You can feel the excitement of these experts about what they are discovering.

Discovery is just the right word for John Ratey, a Harvard professor of medicine. He wrote that those exploring this new field "feel as Balboa must have when he first saw the Pacific Ocean: we don't yet know the full meaning of what we are seeing. ...but we do know it means the beginning of a new age."[4]

Now, before I dive into the details of this a bit—and fear not, I'm going to try and explain all this in entirely understandable terms—I want to tell you what the conclusion of the matter is. I want to tell you the most important part of all of this and why I am so excited about what we are learning in interpersonal neuroscience. Here it is the simplest terms:

1. We are made for relationships.

2. Our relationships actually grow our brains, which in turn influences how we think, feel, and act, thus shaping our lives.

3. Good relationships can have the same medicating effect as good medicine on our brains and our bodies. Bad relationships have the same medicating effect as bad medicine.

Pretty amazing, isn't it? These sound like truths you might hear in a sermon at church or in a marriage seminar. Yet what I've just said is a conclusion of science—of neuroimaging and the most hardcore and stringent scientific research. The insights we are gaining are helping us to heal trauma and to guide people into healthy living, good habits, and vibrant, life-giving relationships.

DISCARDED DOCTRINES

You might be wondering why all this is so surprising and new. Relationships are as old as Adam and Eve. How is it that science seems just to be discovering what human beings have been living out for millennia?

Well, the truth is that science has long made certain assumptions, and these assumptions have shaped what we thought we knew about the brain. Scientists call these assumptions "doctrines."

The first of these doctrines was that the brain was a closed system, that it was controlled in large part by genetic and biological processes and not by outside forces. According to this belief or doctrine, the only way to influence the brain was through neurochemistry—medicines, basically—or other measures like diet and exercise.

The second belief or doctrine of most brain scientists was

that the mind was simply a product of the brain like smoke is a product of fire. The one came from the other. This meant that if you wanted to change some part of your being or if you suffered from some form of mental health problem like depression or anxiety, you had to turn solely to the medical profession for help. According to this assumption, if the brain controlled the mind, fixing the brain fixed the mind and thus behavior. This idea has been behind huge portions of modern psychology and psychiatry—until recently.

This last idea is so pervasive that it has even crept into Christian culture. You've likely heard Christians make a sharp distinction between physical problems and spiritual problems. Challenges like clinical depression and anxiety disorders are viewed as physical problems or chemical imbalances that require medical treatment. But resentment, unforgiveness, pessimism, sexual addiction, and relationship problems are often seen as spiritual problems. The answers for these are said to be reading the Scriptures, prayer, fellowship, and pastoral guidance.

Thank God for Christian leaders who did the best they could under these assumptions. Yet now, with the miracle of new brain scan technology, we've learned that both of these assumptions are flawed. The brain is not a closed system. The brain does not produce the mind like a fire produces smoke. Instead, the brain is relational; it feeds off and grows through the relational interactions we have in life. And some more great news is that the mind can change or shape the brain. So the only kind way to say it is that the two defining dogmas of brain study for years are now crumbling.

NEW DOCTRINES, NEW DAY

Instead of these outdated doctrines or assumptions, interpersonal neuroscience has made three new incredible and overlapping discoveries—discoveries that I assure you are going to change the way we live.

First, a growing number of neuroscientists now believe that the mind and the brain are separate but related entities that interact with each other and influence one another. This is far different from the old fire-and-smoke analogy. Smoke doesn't change fire; it is produced by fire. When scientists thought of the mind as only a product of the brain, they were insisting that we view human behavior only in chemical and physical terms.

However, the new understanding that the mind and the brain are separate and influence each other leads to some exciting outcomes. For example, it means not only that we can change the mind by changing the brain (through such things as medication, diet, and exercise) but also that we can change the brain by changing the mind and behavior (through changing our relational patterns, learning new ways of thinking, and practicing spiritual disciplines like meditation, prayer, silence, solitude, and so on).

Let me tell you that this opens up astonishing possibilities. It means that we aren't limited to medicines and within-the-body solutions to human behavioral problems. Instead, we can also use the mind and behavior to change the brain and thus fix behavioral problems with solutions outside the body, solutions that are possible for every human being. Part of the thrilling truth of these discoveries is that they align with biblical teaching and put healing possibilities back into the hands of God's people and the church.

A second exciting discovery by neuroscientists is that the brain is not fixed at an early age and then closed forever afterward. Instead, new research is revealing that the adult brain has amazing powers of neuroplasticity, much like that seen in a child's brain.[5] Now we know that the brain can rewire itself, that new experiences target and challenge specific neural circuits and thus, in a sense, remake the brain. This is good news for people dealing with every type of mental and emotional problem, and it reinforces the biblical idea of renewing the mind.

> Increasingly, research is confirming that interaction with other human beings has a biological effect on us. This means that our relationships change our brains; they change our behavior and condition the way we experience the world and even God. #focusonthefuture

Yet the third and most exciting discovery scientists are making has to do with the tremendous impact of relationships on the brain. Increasingly, research is confirming that interaction with other human beings has a biological effect on us.[6] This means that our relationships change our brains; they change our behavior and condition the way we experience the world and even God.

OUR RELATIONAL BRAINS

I don't want to get too technical, but let me explain this last point in greater detail since it is such a thrilling discovery. Consider for a moment the experience of telling your life story and then feeling understood by another person. Sounds pretty simple, doesn't it? But we now know that this experience of feeling empathy from someone else produces a calming effect in one's limbic system that is similar to the effects of anxiety drugs like Ativan.[7] Also, to talk about previously unexpressed, emotionally charged experiences challenges the brain to use the powerful, integrative neural circuits of the middle prefrontal cortex, which is involved in helping us learn how to calm our strong emotions, gain flexibility and perseverance, and master our most trouble-some impulses.

This middle prefrontal region is also involved in *mindsight*, a term psychiatrist Dr. Dan Siegel coined to refer to our capacity to perceive and understand our own minds and the minds of others.[8] It is a crucial ability because it provides the platform for fulfilling the Golden Rule. If I can't imagine the mindset and thinking of another person, and if I'm not able to understand even my own mindset, then I won't be able to "do to others what [I] would have them do to [me]."[9] Mindsight is the key to treating others with compassion and understanding, which this middle prefrontal region controls. So our relationships condition our minds for how we will treat others and relate to the world.

These same dynamics help us experience God as another mind, someone with whom we can converse and collaborate through prayer and meditation. This is all the gift of mindsight, which in turn develops within the context of secure attachment relation-ship experiences.

Interestingly, the brain is most open to developing this capacity within the first four to six years of life, but it can be cultivated across the lifespan. Without mindsight, our spiritual walk may become quite superficial, rigid, and mechanical. Individuals with impaired mindsight tend to become stuck in the rut of sin management–based spirituality, having very little sense of Jesus Christ, the Holy Spirit, and God the Father as real persons with emotions, intentions, and thoughts or as beings who are open and responsive to prayer.

Interestingly, research has consistently found that individuals who struggle with chronic, unremitting depression have notable deficits in mindsight and, as a result, have very little understanding of what and why others feel and behave the way they do.[10] They also have very little understanding of how their behavior affects the way others feel and relate to them. Consequently, they tend to feel chronically helpless about their ability to change their relationships, and they become persistently sad, hopeless, and pessimistic about the future. However, new treatments target these prefrontal regions of the brain remarkably effectively in individuals who have failed to respond to any other treatments, including multiple medication trials and even traditional cognitive behavior therapy in combination with medication.[11]

These three new understandings granted by neuroscience are more than just new tools in the hands of therapists. They are entirely new windows on human behavior. They reveal the truth about our minds and brains, aligning with what Scripture says about how we function on the inside and how our outer lives can shape our inner lives, even biologically.

Let me go a bit further here and focus particularly on this central matter of relationships. The core truth is that the mind is relational. In fact, it is dependent on the presence of relationships. From the moment of our birth, our neurons fire and form not just because of genetic patterns but in response to all the interactions we have with other people. We know this now because imaging allows us to watch the brain work when humans respond to other humans. What does this mean? It means that our relationships are helping to wire our brains at the most basic biological level.

Think about it. Every interaction we have from the moment we are born causes electrochemical communication to pass from neuron to neuron in our brains. This happens millions of times during the thousands of relational interactions we experience. Patterns form. Pathways in the brain take shape. Entire biological systems come into place. In other words, our brains are being wired, formed, conditioned, and trained because, as scientists are learning, the experience of the mind changes the brain—even helps to make the brain.

Imagine, then, the brain of a child forming and being conditioned. In a loving home with engaged parents and an environment of safety, nurture, play, learning, and care, a child's brain is quite literally patterned and trained by the experience. A mostly happy, engaged, secure, and intelligent person is the result. Imagine also a home and early life of neglect, abuse, and trauma. The brain is being patterned by this experience too, as is the whole personality. Thus, a damaged person is sent out into the world to respond in unhealthy ways.

Now, think about the significance of parenting, family, and more. In short, from our earliest days of life, relationships wire our brains, either by healthiness or unhealthiness.

THE POWER OF LOVING TOUCH

Now that we've digested this overview of how exciting new brain scan technology is changing our understanding of human behavior, let's get practical. Let's look at some typical human ways of interacting that we are learning have a tremendous impact on our brains, our minds, and thus our behavior. Remember that I've been saying all along in this book that most of the habits and practices that make a huge difference in people's lives are very simple and very doable. Well, let me confirm this now that we understand the gifts of interpersonal neuroscience.

If you are like me, you just want to hold, hug, and love on an adorable baby, like my granddaughter, Olivia. It's natural, isn't it? All this is simply part of how we love, particularly how we love children.

New research from the Nationwide Children's Hospital in Columbus, Ohio, is showing us that the simple act of hugging babies during their developmental period is such a powerful experience that it "triggers their brains to grow, and thus become smarter."[12] Pretty amazing, isn't it? Yet it makes perfect sense in light of what we are learning from interpersonal neuroscience: our brains are relational, and our interactions with other people help to wire our brains and significantly impact how they grow.

The study involved 125 babies, some born preterm and others born full-term. Researchers "analyzed how light physical touch affects their brain development, as well as their perception, cognition, and social development." The thrilling results showed that "supportive experiences, such as breastfeeding, skin-to-skin care, affectionate hugs," and similar types of loving touch caused the children's brains "to develop faster and more healthily."[13] Researchers found that although premature babies generally had a lower brain response to gentle physical contact, those who received regular gentle touch from parents and healthcare workers had a somewhat stronger response. They stressed that "making sure that premature children receive positive, supportive touch...is essential to help their brains respond to gentle touch in ways similar to those of [full-time] babies."[14]

The lead researcher in this study, Dr. Nathalie Maitre, concluded that the simplest of body contact with babies—from rocking them to simply stroking or patting them lovingly— "makes a significant difference in the development of their brains."[15] Given what we know today from interpersonal neuroscience, this makes perfect sense.

Conversely, treating a child harshly or painfully has the opposite effect of loving contact. Harsh touch inhibits brain responses. It slows brain growth and often causes any growth that does occur to be unhealthy. Lower brain function and utility can result—all common in abused, neglected children or those simply exposed to unloving contact.[16]

THE NEUROBIOLOGY OF SHAME

Now, let's take this further. Because we can scan brains to track specific responses and specific emotions, we can also see how certain debilitating emotions take hold of us and thus how we can more easily break free from these crippling forces.

Let's take the force of shame as an example. We all deal with shame at times in our lives, but it deeply impacts some of us. For more than a few of us, this deep feeling stays with us for long periods and proves profoundly harmful. It can also trigger other negative emotions and even lead us into destructive behavior.

Dr. Curt Thompson, a board-certified Christian psychiatrist, has studied this force of shame with the benefits of interpersonal neurobiology. He teaches that shame has a unique neurobiology. You've probably never thought about this when you were feeling shame or helping someone through a season of shame. Yet we have to remember what we are learning today about relationships and the wiring of the brain. All strong emotions, particularly unhealthy ones, have their own neurobiology, their own tracking, and their own ways of working in the brain. This is good news because we can use the insights we gain to set people free.

To understand this unique neurobiology of shame, I'll need to get a bit technical for a moment. From a scientific perspective, the mind does the job of regulating the flow of energy and information that moves from neuron to neuron through the magnificent organ we call the brain.[17] Shame interrupts this natural flow of energy and information and produces a unique set of dysfunctions. Let me allow Dr. Thompson to speak for himself:

> Shame has a tendency to disrupt this process of "regulating the flow of energy and information" by effectively disconnecting various functions of the mind from one another, leaving each domain of the mind as cut off from

one another as we feel ourselves to be disconnected from other people.[18]

This is fascinating and immensely helpful. Amazingly, as one reviewer of Dr. Thompson's book noted, "there is a biological correspondence between toxic shame and the brain." This kind of shame creates "an observable pathology of disconnection in the brain."[19] It cuts off one section of the mind from another. In other words, toxic shame creates in the biology of the brain exactly what it is creating in the life of a shame-filled person: brokenness, disconnection, and exclusion.

Now, "the bad news is that shame is stubborn" and not easily erased. It can be deeply rooted in the brain by childhood experiences that have left their imprint biologically. Since these early experiences "are foundational," it can be "difficult to undo the foundation."[20]

Yet now comes the great insight of the new science. Since the brain and the mind are separate but influence each other, we can deploy the mind to help rewire the brain. Remember, we are learning that the brain is more flexible throughout life than we have believed before. So now we understand that healthy practices can help rewire the brain. What kind of practices exactly? Biblical practices. Powerful spiritual practices like "Christian fellowship, bearing one another's burdens, confession of sin, loving and accepting one another in authentic relationships"—all things Christians are meant to be doing anyway.[21] Now we know that these have tremendous therapeutic value, that they can make a huge difference in healing lives.

I love the way Dr. Thompson summarizes all this in light of how shame is an enemy that comes to destroy us and how spiritual community is much of the answer:

> We cannot thrive on our own....Shame's mission is to disintegrate all institutions in the same way it intends to disintegrate individuals, and isolation is no small part of its tactical arsenal....There is no "Jesus and me" option. There is only "Jesus and us."[22]

OUR RELATIONAL FUTURE

Now, let me ask you to remember that the entire purpose of this book is to help us focus on the future. I'm trying to help us think about what is coming and prepare ourselves to face it as effective, wise people of God. It may sound odd for me to say it this way, but our future is relational, and our healthy relationships are the answer to a great deal that traumatizes our generation.

It wouldn't have been necessary to say such a thing in most previous generations. Relationships seemed almost automatic. Usually, families were large. Members of such families, even extended families, lived together most of their lives. Then there was the tribe or the village. You needed to be in community to survive. You needed to band together, and out of this essential closeness came vital relationships. Communities were tight. Love and laughter, storytelling and music, dancing and celebration were all part of the rituals of life. Life was too dangerous to be a loner.

In short, in many ways people were more connected in earlier generations because the opportunity for relationships was abundant. Given what we now know from interpersonal neuroscience, we can see why people at least appeared healthier. They had meaningful interactions with other human beings from the moment they were born. They lived in a tight-knit relational world, and they belonged to a loving group of people. To put it in modern terms, their brains were encouraged to grow. Strong, positive relationships fired their neurons. All the factors of healthy brain growth were present, from loving touch to play to verbal interaction. Yet keep in mind, relationships were the key.

Now, why have I taken us back into history? It is because even though today we are armed with the insights of modern brain science and can start realizing the vital power of our relationships anew, the truth is that we are also living in a relationally challenged world. We have enemies, so to speak, that we must face if we are going to have the relationships that heal us, fulfill us, and make us healthy, godly human beings. In short, we have a battle to fight for a relational life and a relational future.

THE REWIRING OF SOCIAL MEDIA

We are all grateful, I'm sure, for the blessings of modern social media. I doubt any of us want to see it done away with. So many good things come into our lives from digital technology and the social media that springs from it. But when we understand how vital relationships are, how they can help to heal the trauma of our age, then we also have to be concerned about what social media is doing to us and what a challenge our digital lives are to our relational lives.

One level of concern, certainly, is the sheer distraction factor. We all know what it is like for a family to gather in the same room with everyone on devices instead of being present with each other. We see this everywhere we go. I have a friend who recently went to a baseball game. When cameras began showing people from the crowd on the gigantic digital screen near the scoreboard, most of the people shown were too busy on their devices even to know that they were on camera and to wave and laugh as others did. This is the way it is everywhere these days, and those of us who understand the vital importance of loving relationships and human connections need to push back on this trend toward chronic distraction.

Yet another even scarier trend is happening because of social media, and it has to do with our brains. Again, modern interpersonal neuroscience is giving us astonishing insights that can help us fight against one of the great perils of our age. You see, as we've been learning here, "the brain is a social organ."[23] It is the reason people want to connect, and it is also the reason social media has such appeal to us. We are made for relationships, and so we seek relationships however we can get them, even digitally through social media. The problem we face, though, is that like all human interactions, social media is rewiring our brains. It is shaping us as we use it, and this may not be a good thing.[24] Let me explain.

Dr. Dan Siegel, psychiatry professor at the UCLA School of Medicine, explains that when you are actually with another human being, you experience him or her fully. You make eye contact. You note facial expressions. You take in, even subconsciously, the person's posture, tone of voice, and intensity. Even his or her timing and gestures are signals that your brain is processing to understand, relate to, and communicate with that person. Psychologists often speak of these seven signals in human relationships and communication, so you might want to memorize them: eye contact, facial expressions, tone of voice, postures, gestures, timing, and intensity.[25]

Now, while social media can bring people a bit closer together in some ways, the truth is that it lacks *all* of these seven signals of up-close human interaction. When you are just texting or writing an email, you are using only the verbal part of your brain. You aren't receiving and sending these seven signals that are part of our normal interactions with each other.[26]

Since we know all human interaction develops the brain in some way, the question is, What is social media doing to our brains?

When we are with people and communicating fully, Dr, Siegel says, we are activating the right side or hemisphere of the brain. This is the part of the brain that sends and receives the nonverbal signals we've been talking about. This right side also connects to the brain's lower regions, which connect to our body and emotions. So, in typical, present, face-to-face communication with other people, we activate and develop the brain's right side, the part that is close to our bodies and emotions.[27] This is, of course, wonderful and part of the way God intended it.

The problem is that when we do social media by the hour and when this is the primary way we connect with people, we are using mainly the verbal part of our brain or the left hemisphere. This left side is verbal and logistical. Since it is the left side of our brains, it is removed from the part of the brain that connects to the body, emotions, and full interactions with other people.[28]

Dr. Siegel contends that if we develop mainly the left hemisphere of the brain to the neglect of the right, we can diminish the parts of us that connect us with other people. We can begin to experience the world in superficial ways. The right side of the brain also controls autobiographical memory, so Dr. Siegel is concerned that people who are addicted to social media can even get to a point where they don't know what is going on inside themselves. [29]

What really confirms his concerns is a trend that we counselors and therapists are seeing and that the major media has frequently mentioned recently, especially as a result of the COVID-19 lockdown. This is that younger generations—millennials in particular—are having less sex than previous generations. They live very distracted lives and have too much on their minds to connect with their spouses physically as fully as they should—all due mainly to social media.[30] This is precisely what Dr. Siegel is saying: social media is rewiring brains, moving people toward the verbal and logistical side of their brains and away from parts that send and receive human communication signals, away from their emotional and physical lives, and even away from the knowledge of their inner selves.

It would be going too far to say that modern social media is making us robots, but this is an image that might help us understand how social media is rewiring our brains—toward words and logic, away from the human, the emotional, and the physical. Away even from self-knowledge. Hmmm. Sounds to me like the robots I've seen in the movies!

THE CONVERGENCE AND THE CRISIS

In all that we've seen here about how we are made for relationships and how relationships even serve to wire our brains for good and bad, two conflicting facts are creating a major social crisis in our age.

The first fact is how social we are. Again, scientists tell us that the brain is a social organ. We are learning that our relationships help make us who we are. We are, as we have long been told, social beings.

The second fact is the disturbing way devotion to social media is capable of rewiring our brains and impacting our personalities. Relying on texts, emails, and posts for relating to other people emphasizes only one part of the brain—the logical and verbal. The other part of our brain is not challenged as it would be if we were actually with people. So the parts of us that are emotional, physical, and self-aware weaken and grow distant, as the brain scientists indicate. This moves us away from being genuinely able to relate to the world and others in a full and meaningful way.

Now, if we hold these two facts in our hands—we are social beings, but social media moves us away from deep relationships and experiences of the world—what would we expect to find happening around us? What feeling would we expect people, the young and social media–minded in particular, to be consumed with? The answer is loneliness. It only makes sense. And this is precisely what we do find. Indeed, it is one of the mounting crises of our age.

Researchers are confirming this almost daily. Among the most "wired" online age group—millennials, meaning those born between 1981 and 1996[31]—life ought to be good. They are well educated. They are among the most prosperous of all their age-mates throughout history. They should be feeling the joy of starting families and moving up the career ladder. But a growing number of them don't feel this way. A recent poll revealed that "30 percent of millennials say they feel lonely." This is the highest percentage of any generation living today.[32]

Not only do three in ten millennials say they feel lonely, but it gets worse. Some 27 percent "said they had 'no close friends,' 30 percent said they have 'no best friends,' and 25 percent said they have no acquaintances," while 22 percent stated they had no friends at all. So not only are millennials—the most social media–engaged age group—feeling lonely, but a considerable portion of them also find they don't have close, meaningful rela-tionships. "In comparison, just 16 percent of Gen Xers" (the age group between baby boomers and millennials) "and 9 percent of baby boomers say they have no friends."[33]

So, why would a quarter of an entire generation say they lack friends? And perhaps more importantly, what is going to happen as millennials age, since experts tell us that loneliness tends to increase the older a generation gets?

Allow me to stick with the negative news a bit more to illus-trate the good news I want you to know. You see, it isn't just the millennials who are feeling alone. Americans in general report a crisis of friendship.

Recently, one of our nation's largest health insurers, Cigna, reported the results of a study revealing that most Americans feel "lonely, left out and not known."[34] Similar studies by the Barna Group showed that "the majority of adults has anywhere between two and five close friends (62%), but one in five regularly or often feels lonely."[35]

Adding to this, while most Americans see their neighbors weekly (39 percent) or daily (28 percent), 37 percent say these interactions are friendly, polite greetings that do not usually lead to more meaningful connections. In other words, Americans see and greet their neighbors, but their neighbors seldom become friends of any depth.[36]

An interesting part of Barna's research reveals that when it comes to friendship, opposites don't attract. People tend to be friends with folks who are like them, not different. Americans' preference for befriending people who are like them "is true for religious beliefs (62% similar, 38% different), race or ethnicity (74% vs. 26%), income (56% vs. 44%), education level (63% vs. 37%), social status (70% vs. 30%), political views (62% vs. 38%) and life stage (69% vs. 31%)."[37]

I should add that this same Barna report states that "evangelicals are less likely than most to have friends who are different than them." This is especially true when it comes to friends who share their religious beliefs (91 percent similar), friends who have the same ethnicity (88 percent similar), and friends who share their political views (86 percent similar).[38] In short, when it comes to friendship, evangelicals in America just aren't reaching out to people who are unlike them.

At a time when society is suffering relational wounds and loneliness, when technology and social trends are rending the fabric of our relationships, churches can offer the very relational interactions that brain scientists tell us are the keys to healing and restoration.
#focusonthefuture

Where does all this lead us? If we are considering the future and both the challenges and the blessings that it brings, the insights of interpersonal neuroscience promise wonderful things. We see how vital relationships are for happy lives. We understand that our brains can change—not just in our early days but throughout our lifetimes. We also find that habits of the mind and body can bring health to the brain and thus to our lives.

Yet we also have to realize that we are living in a society that is increasingly disconnected, increasingly damaging itself through social media, and increasingly feeling lonely and friendless. This is tragic both because it is painful and because of something the new brain science is teaching us: relationships are the key to healing trauma. Community—particularly Christian community with its devotion to prayer, confession, openness, vulnerability, service, and investment in others—is more and more being understood as a bulwark against the traumatizing culture in which we live.

There are tremendous opportunities for Christian churches here. At a time when society is suffering relational wounds and loneliness, when technology and social trends are rending the fabric of our relationships, churches can offer the very relational interactions that brain scientists tell us are the keys to healing and restoration. Of course, social scientists are speaking just at a psychological level. But we Christians know that we have not only the mental benefits of our faith and practices to offer but also the love of God and the power of the Holy Spirit. We really can be the healing force we are called to be in our traumatized generation. We can make the difference our age needs and that we believers in Jesus long to be in our time.

WHO IS REALLY WITH US?

Because we are talking about the future and how we can prepare for it, I've been speaking primarily in macro terms. I've told you about brain science and studies with babies and trends with our youth and how most people in our generation are feeling about having friends and community. Yet for me to truly do my job in these pages and help you prepare for the challenges of our age, I need to speak to you in very personal terms.

Let me start with a story. A few years ago, my son, Zach, and I took a fishing trip into the Alaskan wild. It was enchanting. Let me try to describe it. Our site was deep in the thick bush tundra of the Alaskan Iliamna River area. Soaring, snowcapped mountains surrounded us. The region we were heading into was remote. There were no stores, medical facilities, or McDonald's. Nothing. In fact, there were few people. Yet Zach and I were acutely aware that we were not alone. Brown bears, moose, salmon, and arctic char populated this magnificent land and its beautiful, glacier-fed streams.[39]

We had a blast! We fished together and laughed—a lot! We got a little confused on where we were on the map more than once and were barely concerned. Majestic mountains towered all around us and somehow made us feel safe. Our time was rich with fireside chats, games of horseshoes and cornhole, and, of course, fish stories, which were more like fish lies really. I won't tell you how much we ate, but trust me, our meals at the lodge were sumptuous. In short, we played hard, connected deeply, rested well, and refreshed thoroughly. It was as though we had escaped to another, more glorious planet than the one we usually lived on.

Let me tell you part of the reason all this was possible. Though the lodge was fantastic and the food was, as I've said, almost overwhelming, the internet service was spotty at best. We found this maddening at first. Then it became a blessing. We began focusing on each other more and drinking in the call of the wild. We were there only a day or two before we realized we no longer cared about internet service. We simply never used it. Our minds were free, and our souls were able to soar in those magnificent surroundings. We ended up actually thanking God for bad wireless service!

I don't want you to misunderstand me. I'm obviously grateful for modern technology and for the redemptive use of the internet. We all are. It is a gift of God. What I want you to see, though, is that in just a few days in the Alaska wild I came to realize how bound I was to being online. Many executives of major technological companies even acknowledge that device use is becoming addictive and has mental health implications.[40]

I'm thankful for this level of honesty from the heads of global tech firms because they are right. Our devices can be dangerous to us. As I mentioned in chapter 4, half of all teenagers "feel addicted" to their mobile devices. In fact, 78 percent of teenagers feel the need to check their mobile devices on an hourly basis. And their parents are nearly as bad, for 69 percent of this group polled say they also check their phones at least once per hour.[41]

What is driving this behavior? I think it is the factor now referred to as FOMO, "fear of missing out." We cannot seem to shake the nagging sense that everyone else is participating in an amazing experience and we are the only ones who are not a part of it. The only way to ensure we are not missing out is to feverishly check our social media feeds—a habit that quickly becomes an obsession. This kind of obsession must be the reason that 47 percent of adults admit to sending or reading text messages while behind the wheel of a car and 44 percent of adults report having been a passenger when the driver used his or her phone in a way that put people in danger.[42] What else but obsession would explain such behavior?

As hazardous as such behavior is, more dangerous still is what happens to our bodies and minds as a result of our device addictions. Recent studies suggest a correlation between increased phone use and a rise in depression and suicide among teenagers. Teens who spent five or more hours per day on devices were nearly twice as likely to consider suicide than teens who spent only one hour.[43]

The bottom line is that our sense of being left out is crushing us; we feel we are somehow falling behind people whom, in many cases, we don't even know. This is what our devices scream to us, and in our fear, we allow an obsession to settle into our souls that kills our relationships and threatens to drive our young to kill themselves. It is time for the madness to stop. I share the concern of my good friend, Dr. Sylvia Frejd, that in the future, it will be almost impossible for students of this generation to get off their devices, because their devices will be their lives.[44]

Our devices are tools. We should use them to connect with others and to enhance our lives. Yet when they drive us, when their absence fills us with fear of being left out and their presence awakens obsessions in our souls, then we are opening the door to destruction. Heed my words, please. Be smart in your use of technology. Be honest about the benefits and downsides. There are plenty of both. Put your devices in their proper place so that you own technology and it does not own you.

Let me take you back to the wilderness with me. The weather is intoxicating. The river lulls your mind to peaceful daydreaming. The ways of the fish and bear feel one with the rhythms of your soul and all of life. The people with you seem closer, more open, more accessible. You are inspired, refreshed, energized. You realize that the hand of God has painted a glorious canvas, and nothing about social media can ever compare with it.

As we were reveling in the wonder of creation, a friend led a devotional time for us one morning. He recounted the story from Acts 18:9–11 of the apostle Paul having a vision from the Lord. The Lord spoke to Paul, saying, "I am with you." It reminded me of Matthew 28:20, when Jesus says, "I am with you always." In the original language, these words could also be read as, "I am with you all the days."[45]

My mind immediately went to the false comfort of our electronic devices. We have them with us nearly all the time. We use them so often and so habitually that we are literally rewiring our brains. Yet what we know, and what God's words to Paul confirm, is that only God can truly be with us "all the days." To be fulfilled, to cease feeling alone and empty, we have to turn to our God and tame our need for our devices. We have to silence the noise and recover the riches of God, His creation, and the people He has put around us. This is when genuine life really occurs for us.

Armed with the insights of Scripture and interpersonal neuroscience, we have a bright future—if we make it bright! What amazing news it is that our relationships can help heal us. What glorious liberation it is to learn that our spiritual disciplines as devoted Christians can serve to reset our brains and reorder our lives—not just in spiritual matters but in all our behavior. Also, how thrilling it is to know that as wounding and traumatizing as our society is, Christian churches can be healing agents, bringing hurting people into the grace of God, the love of God, the power of God, and the mysteries of restoration He has built into our amazing brains. Truly, we can live out some of the most magnificent words in the Bible:

> Two are better than one, because they have a good return for their labor: if either of them falls down, one can help the other up. But pity anyone who falls and has no one to help them up. Also, if two lie down together, they will keep warm. But how can one keep warm alone? Though one may be overpowered, two can defend themselves. A cord of three strands is not quickly broken.
> —ECCLESIASTES 4:9–12

CHAPTER 6

STANDING GUARD FOR
THE NEXT GENERATION

I T WAS ONE of the most harrowing moments of my young life. I'll never forget it.

It occurred not far from our family home in rural Pennsylvania. Behind the parsonage in which we lived in those days was a vast buckwheat field, and just below it was an old strip-mining hole. As controversial as this kind of mining might be today, we kids loved it because it left a huge pit filled with water. It was like having a private lake or pond, all concealed by the locust trees that surrounded it.

We also loved it because it was filled with chub, which is pretty much a garbage fish, not very good for eating and mainly used for bait. Yet we had a ball fishing for chub. My friends and I found them exciting to catch and competed as fiercely as any professional fishermen ever have!

Adults had warned us to be careful, mainly because the ledges around the water were made of shale. They were brittle and very slippery when wet, and since the banks around the water were high, it meant nothing but danger if someone fell in.

In short, we had no business being down there on the upper

side of the stripping cut. We knew this, and nothing confirmed it like that day I'll never forget. While we were fishing and horsing around, my friend Joe either fell or jumped into the water. He may have intended it as a prank, but if so, it wasn't funny for long. He soon realized that the water was deep, the sides were slick, and he had no way to get himself out of the watery blackness that threatened to swallow him.

I was watching from the banks with my other friends, all just young kids. If we thought at first Joe was messing around, that thought evaporated quickly. We soon realized he was drowning. We were paralyzed for a moment and then began screaming for help. As we did, we realized how isolated we all were. Down in a hole and surrounded by trees as we were, no one could hear us. It didn't help that the mining site was on the other side of a buckwheat field. We screamed as loudly as we could while trying to reach him—as the guilt that we had ever put ourselves in that position washed over us.

I want you to picture the scene. Joe is drowning. His mop of red hair is bobbing up and down in the dark, shale-colored water. Fear and then resignation register in his eyes. The rest of us scream from the shale banks, realizing our friend is about to die right in front of us.

At that moment an older boy named Jake appeared. Thank God for him. He had been out in that buckwheat field for some reason. He heard our screams and came running. He bounded through the surrounding trees and down the crumbling shale before diving into the water. Somehow he got to Joe, grabbed a fistful of red hair, and dragged that drowning boy to the side before pretty much throwing him up onto the bank. Then, he carefully crawled out of the water and up the shale to safety. He was older and stronger, able to jump into a rescue the rest of us wouldn't have survived.

He saved Joe's life that day. That is the plain and simple truth. It was a rescue if I've ever seen one, and that moment comes to mind every time I hear the word *rescue*.

RESCUE OF A GENERATION

I tell you this unsettling story because I want us to focus together on the word *rescue*. Our young, our children, need rescuing today—as surely as Joe needed rescuing from those black, enveloping waters in that mining pit. In the same way, our young are being swallowed by the abuse, pain, addictions, neglect, depression, and lies of our age.

> I want to sound a trumpet call for an older generation of those who see the times clearly and know what they need to do, who are willing to armor up and engage the battle for the next generation. #focusonthefuture

Who is going to rescue them? We are—you and me and thousands like us. In fact, in this chapter, I want to call out warriors who will stand guard for the next generation. Warrior dads. Warrior moms. Warrior uncles and aunts and brothers and sisters and church members and community members. I want to sound a trumpet call for an older generation of those who see the times clearly and know what they need to do, who are willing to armor up and engage the battle for the next generation.

Where do I get this warrior language? I get it from one of my favorite passages about the relationship between two generations. It comes from Psalm 127:

Like arrows in the hand of a warrior, so are the children
of one's youth. Happy is the man who has his quiver full

of them; they shall not be ashamed, but shall speak with
their enemies in the gate.

—PSALM 127:4–5, NKJV

The imagery is powerful here: it depicts the older generation
as a skilled and capable warrior and his children as arrows. The
warrior/father not only has a quiver full of them, but he is firing
those arrows/children into the next generation. Those arrows are
prepared. They are in the warrior/father's hands. They are not
ashamed. They speak—some translations say "contend"—with
their enemies in the gates. In other words, as the children fight
the battles of their generation, they have already been prepared
and skillfully deployed by their warrior/parents and the whole
warrior/adult generation that sent them forth.

How desperately we need to reclaim this vision of generational
responsibility today! How very much we need to battle for the
young so that they in turn can fight the battles of their lives and
be victorious to the glory of God!

Let me tell you a secret concealed in this verse. It is an image
I hope you will carry with you always when you think of our
calling to care for and wisely deploy the next generation.

An often-used illustration tells us that when warriors went out
to cut the wood for new arrows, they naturally cut from wood
that was young and green and as yet unseasoned. Once they had
trimmed the unnecessary and unhelpful parts of the wood away,
they tied the young arrows—the newly cut, green wood—to the
finished, seasoned, tested arrows. This was so that while the new
arrows dried, they would be as straight and as firm as the older
arrows. Lashed together, the young arrows would dry out and
take final form. Only when they were ready to be notched and
have an arrowhead attached would the warrior unlash the old
arrows from the young. Only when they were ready. Only when

they had taken on the nature of the mature and battle-tested arrows.

You see, the preparation of the young in this illustration was accomplished by binding them tightly to the older and fully formed. The duty of the older, in one sense, was to "come around" the younger and protect them, making them ready by their presence. The preparation was accomplished by being close, being bound, being the model, and imparting what the young needed.

This is our calling today. Our children need rescue, and then they need to be protected and prepared by mature ones coming around them and imparting what we have. We saw in chapter 5, about brain science, that relationships are therapy, that relationships can help heal and restore, rewire and reposition. This is what our children need today, and we cannot do it from a distance. We must invest in the young, offering the relationships we are meant to provide in all the roles we play in their lives—parent, relative, friend, pastor, coach, teacher, church member, community member, and model of noble manhood or womanhood.

I'm thrilled to sound the trumpet call for this older warrior generation. I'm thrilled to do it because of what it will mean for our traumatized young. I'm also thrilled to do it for what it will mean for our nation. Yet like true warriors, we have to look carefully at the opposition we face. The enemy is fierce, and he is effective. Tragically, he has already gained much ground, but he can be challenged and defeated.

THE SPIRIT OF OUR TIMES

The most significant source of opposition we face in standing guard for the next generation is in a spirit or an attitude that plagues our own generation. Let me use a biblical story to illustrate this, and then I'll show you how the statistics bear out what I'm saying.

Consider with me the story found in 2 Kings 20:12–21 of King Hezekiah and the Babylonian envoys. It seems that the Babylonian ruler of those days sent emissaries to Hezekiah. The king welcomed these envoys and showed them all his treasures. The Bible tells us, "There was nothing in his house or in all his dominion that Hezekiah did not show them."[1]

The prophet Isaiah heard about this. He went to Hezekiah and asked what the Babylonians had come for and what they had seen. The king told him, "They have seen all that is in my house; there is nothing among my treasures that I have not shown them."[2]

Then the word of the Lord came to Isaiah. It was a horrible prophecy, and we should consider it in full: "'Behold, the days are coming when all that is in your house, and what your fathers have accumulated until this day, shall be carried to Babylon; nothing shall be left,' says the LORD. 'And they shall take away some of your sons who will descend from you, whom you will beget; and they shall be eunuchs in the palace of the king of Babylon.'"[3]

It was the worst thing Isaiah could have predicted for a king like Hezekiah. All that had been entrusted to him by his fathers would be lost. Nothing would be left. Even worse, his sons would be carried away and castrated, made to be eunuchs in the house of a foreign king. In short, Hezekiah's future was over. All he had and had given birth to would be destroyed.

You would expect Hezekiah to kill himself on the spot at such news. He didn't. Instead, he turned to Isaiah and said, "The word of the LORD you have spoken is good"! Good?! How could he say such a thing? Yet we know why, and it is because the Bible tells us what Hezekiah was thinking: "Will there not be peace and security in my lifetime?"[4]

There it is! The spirit, the attitude that is plaguing our generation. "The future may be lost. All that we are responsible for will be destroyed in future generations. But it is okay because we will have peace and prosperity while we live—no need to worry about what will happen after we are gone."

A preoccupation with our own generation is the first enemy we face if we are going to stand guard for the next generation. It is a preference of our own time, prosperity, and well-being over that of the next generation.

Now, because you are reading this book and you are eager to focus on the future, you may be saying, "I don't feel anything like that! I care deeply about the next generation, and I'm ready to stand guard." Good! I'm glad you think like this, but just so you don't think I'm exaggerating the reach of the enemy, consider this disturbing bit of truth from Stephanie Coontz's marvelous book *The Way We Never Were*. "Twenty-five percent of the people polled in a recent national inquiry into American morality said that for $10 million they would abandon their entire family; a large number of people are evidently willing to do the same thing for free."[5]

Think about this. For the right amount of money, a quarter of Americans would walk away from their families. And, as Coontz said, a considerable portion is willing to do it for free. This is, I'm sorry to say, the spirit of Hezekiah coming upon our generation. "Horrors are going to visit our land and our people, but they will not happen in our lifetime. Why worry? Why stress? Leave the agonies to our children and grandchildren."

These are disturbing attitudes, but they are not surprising in a nation that thinks like many Americans do about abortion. I don't want to dwell on this at length. But if we consider the next generation expendable—if we make it legal to sacrifice that generation to our comforts and needs—then it should be no surprise that many Americans would not be disturbed by visiting catastrophes on the next generation. Nor would they be willing to expend themselves to help the next generation now, to rescue them from the traumas that generation is enduring while it is young.

Consider just for a moment that many in our nation believe in unrestricted abortion—as of 2019, 60 percent do not want *Roe v. Wade* overturned, 25 percent believe abortion should be legal under any circumstances, and 46–52 percent consider them-selves pro-abortion.[6] With this much of the nation holding these attitudes, is it any wonder that our young need rescuing, that we need a warrior generation of parents and leaders to stand guard and assure the future of our children?

THE POWER OF THE FAMILY

The good news is that the solution is within our reach. Change can be made. A turnaround, a rescue, can occur. The answer is as near as the home and the family.

I have to say it once again. Dr. Dobson was right from the beginning. The family is the answer to the vast majority of our social ills. God ordained the home to be the place where hearts and hands were fashioned. God puts a premium on the home. It was the first institution ordained by God, and when it comes to shaping human lives, it is where the action happens. The rescue of the next generation might seem overwhelming, but it is as simple as a return to the home, to relationships, and to loving mothers and fathers and the powerful impartation that loving families naturally produce in the young.

> The rescue of the next generation might seem overwhelming, but it is as simple as a return to the home, to relationships, and to loving mothers and fathers and the powerful impartation that loving families naturally produce in the young. #focusonthefuture

I've always been moved by something I read in the words of Abraham Lincoln. He once said, "All that I am or hope ever to be I get from my mother, God bless her."[7]

This may not sound that unusual. Many great men and women credit their mothers as the inspiration for what they achieved. Yet Lincoln's mother, Nancy, died when young Abraham was only nine years old. Lincoln would not begin showing himself an exceptional man until nearly twenty years later. Apparently, in those first ten years, Nancy Lincoln had such an impact on her son that he credited her with all that he achieved. Though Nancy was poor and lacked a formal education, she loved her boy, narrated the world to him, taught him Bible verses she had memorized, and was always present as her sensitive, gifted, unusual son rose to early manhood. She shaped a man and, in time, a nation, and all in just ten years.[8] This is the power of the family. This is what parents can do, even in the most challenged families, when they simply care and give themselves to their children.

Nancy Lincoln's kind of impact seems hard to achieve in our day. It isn't, really, but the distractions of life and the false values of our age get in the way. I've always thought that the most blessed man in the world is the one who has little noses pressed against the windowpane waiting for him to come home. This is how I grew up. Perhaps you did too. Nothing thrilled me like those powerful words, "Dad's home!"

Thankfully, I have felt what it is like to have a little one nearly dancing around the house at the thrill of me coming home. It is a transforming experience. When my son, Zach, was only two or three years old, I returned home one evening to find my little guy running full speed toward me. I mean, he was running wide open! When he got to me, he stopped and gleefully shouted, "Dad!" Then he looked down at my shoes and said, "Shoes off!"

This moved me because I realized that he was saying, "Dad, come here with me. Be with me."

I don't think I'm taking it too far to say that the main way we rescue the next generation is to answer this heart cry of our children. "Dad. Mom. Be with me. Come here with me." It is the answer, truly, not only for our children but also for our nation.

So when I issue a call for warrior moms and dads, I'm not necessarily asking people to storm out into the streets and start raising a cry for the next generation. This may be necessary at times, but I'm mainly calling for parents and other adults who will be like those older arrows I described—strong, straight, seasoned, and willing to bind themselves to the young to protect them and to help them become what they are meant to be. I am calling for a warrior adult generation who understands the times and knows how to protect the next generation from the ills of our day.

TARGETING A GENERATION

Now, like any good warriors, we need to know what our target is. I can almost picture you as you read this book. It is as though you are in a prebattle briefing, and you are receiving the information necessary for the rescue operations I am asking you to execute. We are excited and motivated, but we need military intelligence for the operation ahead.

Our operation, of course, is the rescue, protection, and nurture of the young generation on the rise today. But what is that generation? Who are they? What do they need?

Let's find out!

We all know that the baby boomer generation, about 73 million strong, was born just after World War II. You may be part of this generation. Then, a generation usually called Generation X came along. If you are part of this generation, you are the children of the boomers, were born from the early 1960s through the 1980s, and are in your forties and fifties today. You may even have grandchildren of your own by now. Boomers and Gen Xers are included in the warrior generation I'm writing to, but our rescue operations are focused on yet another generation.

You might think I'm speaking of the millennials. God knows every generation—the millennials, in particular—needs the help of sound, godly people. Yes, we are called to reach them, but the millennials are not in our homes anymore, not as malleable or under our influence. Scholars often point to the range between 1981 and 1996 as the birth years for the millennials. Though it is hard to believe, the oldest millennials are nearly forty years old now, so they are out in the world already and already shaping our society.

Who, then, is the generation in our homes whom we can still protect, shape, love, and inspire? Experts call them Generation Z. Let me tell you about them.

They were born from 1997 to 2010, through the dawn of the new millennium, and the oldest of them have graduated from college as I write this. Gen Z is known by several other names, including iGen, the app generation, the selfie generation, and even the transgeneration. As you can tell by some of these labels, technology—and the way this generation uses it—has come to define how we perceive Gen Z.

Let's strive for a clearer picture of who they are. In a fantastic article about Gen Z, author Sean McDowell offers several insights into this generation. The first and perhaps the most revealing truth is that they are digital natives.[9] They cannot remember a time when there were no iPhones or iPads. Remember that the iPhone first released in 2007 and the iPad in 2010. This means that from the moment this generation was old enough to hold a device in their hands, they have been swiping and tapping away to navigate an increasingly seductive online world. They are the first generation on earth to be completely native in the digital world. In other words, other generations watched the technology being developed and came to it later in their lives, but Generation Z has always lived in a digital world. It is their native land.

Perhaps in part because of this digital upbringing, Generation Z is passionately entrepreneurial. They are at home in a world served by Uber and Airbnb.[10] Almost every question in their lives can be answered with "There is an app for that." Ordering food and groceries; buying household items, clothing, cars, and houses; streaming music, movies, television shows, news, and church services; and even banking, paying bills, filing tax returns, and seeking medical advice—all things that took earlier generations some effort now require a few pushes of a button on a digital device or talking to an AI persona or smart appliance. It is part of the reason why 54 percent of Gen Zers dream of starting their own businesses.[11]

This entrepreneurial lean, by their own admission, can make them individualistic or self-centered, even selfishly demanding.[12] As one expert says, "Gen Z is used to having everything personalized just for them, from playlists to newsfeeds to product features of all kinds. They've grown up expecting that."[13] If they are not careful and considerate of others, they can quickly expect everything to be a customized fit for them and assume even that other people should revolve around their needs. Another generation might say that what is hard is bad; Generation Z is tempted to believe that anything uncomfortable and not customized specifically for them is bad.

Yet as much as they want the world to conform to their individuality, Gen Zers are also more used to others being different from them than any other American generation. They are, simply put, the most diverse generation in our history. They are one of the last American generations that will be majority white. And they are only 52 percent white as it is.[14] During 2000–2010, in the heart of the Gen Z years, the Hispanic population in the United States "grew at four times the rate of the total population."[15] This generation also grew up with a black American president. They see nearly every variation of skin color and ethnic culture on their devices. They are at home in a racially and ethnically mixed world.[16]

Consistent with their entrepreneurial, customizable approach to life, they are remaking religion in their own image as well. Consider this: In 1966, only 6.6 percent of new college students declared themselves to be unaligned with a religion. Yet in 2015, almost one third, or 29.6 percent, of all new college freshmen claimed not to identify with any traditional religion.[17]

Now, the likelihood is that Generation Z is not necessarily less religious, but they just aren't affiliated with any organized religion.[18] Instead, some Gen Zers curate faiths, combine elements of different faiths they admire, and "do" religion on their own. Some have said that this generation does religion as other generations did jazz music—customizing, breaking from norms, rearticulating, and, ultimately, making new blended religions of their own. It is not uncommon for members of Gen Z to call themselves "Christian Buddhists" or say that they believe in divine destiny, reincarnation, and Zen—three concepts from three different religions.

In their experience, this constant need to customize merges with a murky world devoid of traditional boundaries and definitions. Generation Z is, for lack of a better word, "blurry." Sean McDowell tells us that for this generation "technology has blurred the lines between home and work, study and entertainment, and public and private. Gen Zers have a different experience of family—same-sex households, working moms, stay-at-home dads, three-parent families, and couples choosing not to have kids.... And, of course, gender and romantic identities have become blurry as well."[19] In short, the traditional lines have faded some for this generation, the old definitions kept from them or leached from their experience. Their world is blurry; some would say messy or ill-defined. This has become their reality, and it is profoundly shaping how they intend to live.

They see this blurring of lines as their unique kind of progressivism. The vast majority plan "to get married, have children, and buy a home." Sounds fairly traditional, doesn't it? Add to this that they "are less likely to drink, smoke, and take drugs," which makes them almost appear to hearken back to earlier times and values. Yet they hold politically progressive views on issues like same-sex marriage and the legality of marijuana, abortion, and immigration.[20] As in religion, they are curating cultural beliefs and practices in whole new ways.

This blurring may lead to some of their dysfunctions. Generation Z reports being deeply lonely.[21] Experts tell us that 13 percent of adolescents from ages twelve to seventeen—which places them squarely in the Generation Z range—have had at least one major depressive episode in the past year.[22] Anxiety and depression plague them, in large part due to the fact that they've grown up post-9/11, and terrorism and school shootings like Sandy Hook have become common realities during their lifetimes. Suicide haunts their generation, and the headlines don't help. Many significant figures, like Robin Williams, Anthony Bourdain, and fashion leader Kate Spade, have committed suicide during the lives of Gen Z and raised the specter of a plague of self-harm that pervades this entire young tribe.[23]

Finally, this generation feels, perhaps understandably, constantly overwhelmed.[24] Susanna Schrobsdorff perfectly captured this generation-wide feeling in an article for *Time* magazine when she wrote of the "pervasive sense that being a teenager today is a draining full-time job that includes doing schoolwork, managing a social media identity and fretting about career, climate change, sexism, racism—you name it."[25] Sadly, one survey showed that some 68 percent of this generation feel overwhelmed by nearly everything they do each week.[26] Undoubtedly, this feeling feeds the depression and anxiety that permeate this tribe of over-achievers who never seem to feel caught up, visionaries who never seem to rise to their own expectations, and perfectionists who seldom feel that life meets their demands. Disappointment follows, as does worry, fear, and, ultimately, a debilitating depression.

I imagine as you read this description of Gen Z, you feel much as I do. I love them. I feel compassion for them. I want to tell them God's truth over a good meal. I also want to urge us to keep in mind what we have learned about relationships as therapy. When you ponder the attributes of Generation Z, remember these things:

1. We are all made for relationships.

2. Healthy relationships can have the effect of good medicine.

3. Even later in life, relationships and loving experiences can help to rewire the brain.

4. God is reaching out to every generation all the time, which gives us hope for every generation. It also provides us with a sense of mission to reach them and love them.

Now, there is some fascinating good news in all this information about Gen Z, but allow me to continue describing some of the challenges of this wonderful but troubled tribe we have before us. It will sharpen our sense of mission and help us be more effective as we go to war for them.

First, let me throw some difficult statistics at you. These may shock you, but remember that I do this by way of arming you for standing guard over the young in our midst. Here are some of the dire statistics about this generation—largely Gen Zers—that we have in our lives. All these statistics are from the National Institute of Mental Health:

- 20 percent of youth ages thirteen to eighteen live with a mental health condition.

- 11 percent of youth have a mood disorder.

- 10 percent of youth have a behavior or conduct disorder.

- 8 percent of youth have an anxiety disorder.

- Suicide is the third leading cause of death in youth ages ten to twenty-four, and 90 percent of those who died by suicide had an underlying mental illness.

- 37 percent of students with a mental health condition age fourteen and older drop out of school—the highest dropout rate of any disability group.

- 70 percent of youth in state and local juvenile justice systems have a mental illness.[27]

So, let me round out our picture of Generation Z. They are amazingly gifted. They think in new and creative ways. They dream of what has not yet been, determined to live their lives free from the confinement of social categories. In the future, they will defy strict definitions of political left and right. They will refuse to think in terms of liberal and conservative religion. They will insist upon doing life as jazz, as the music they make while boldly setting out in new directions, taking with them the best of the old and what they believe to be the all-essential new.

Yet this is a deeply troubled generation. They are lonely. They are depressed. They live with agonizing mental disorders and behavioral dysfunctions. They have suffered from our national plague of fatherlessness more than any other generation. In an almost warm but also naive way, they tend to absorb the horrors that fill our headlines into their souls, often speaking of them as though they experienced them firsthand. They feel bullied by life, whether it is the sheer pace of their schedules or the pressure to perform or burdens like student debt. They sense that their parents' generation has betrayed them and left them a damaged world. They don't know how to escape it all, but they are determined not to take any of the previous generation's certainties—whether about morals or religion or gender or politics—as certainties of their own.

They are determined but a bit lost. They are gifted but also unstable. They feign confidence but are, in truth, profoundly needy. They resist what has come before them but also hunger for the good and wholesome that previous generations have known. And, I repeat, God is reaching to them.

A GIFTED GENERATION

I believe that part of the reason God is reaching to this generation—aside from the magnificent fact that He loves each one of them dearly and sent His Son to die for them—is that they are amazingly powerful. They have gifts and vision and skills that are going to allow them to shape the world. This too is part of why we need to go to war for Generation Z.

I'm sure you remember when a gunman shot seventeen people at the Marjory Stoneman Douglas High School in Parkland,

Florida, in February 2018. It was a ghastly experience, part of the plague of school shootings that is traumatizing a generation. Yet do you know what those students at that high school did? They did what Generation Z does—they wept, they grieved, and then they got busy.

Over the next several weeks, those Parkland teens helped to organize one of the most massive youth protests since the Vietnam War. They launched a #NeverAgain movement on social media. Their confrontations with politicians, captured on video, went viral. And in the last couple of years as the oldest of them have come of age, they have begun turning up at the polls in substantial numbers. This too is a mark of Generation Z.

The entire Gen Z response to the Parkland shooting was so impressive that late-night talk show host Stephen Colbert said this on his program: "Someone else may be in power, but this country belongs to them."[28] He was right. And, increasingly, Generation Z knows it.

In fact, in a seminal article in *Forbes* magazine, author Ashley Stahl explains how Generation Z is both influential and defying expectations. Entitled "Why Democrats Should Be Losing Sleep Over Generation Z," Stahl's article contends that while 83 percent of millennials and 85 percent of Generation X describe their views as "quite" or "very liberal," 59 percent of Gen Zers describe their views as "moderate" or "conservative."[29] This, of course, is a surprising reality.

Stahl suggests that much of this may be because, as digital natives, Generation Z gets its information straight from the internet. They aren't molded by institutions, aren't as subject to tradition or conventional information or thinking. This is obvious from the Gen Z attitude toward student debt. While millennials wallow in student debt, Gen Zers "avoid student loans like fire!"[30] As Stahl noted, a 2017 national study by The Center for Generational Kinetics concluded that Gen Z students plan to limit or avoid personal debt, work during college, and save for retirement.[31]

Surprisingly, Gen Z is already rising above its negative branding as a tribe of materialistic consumers. Some 12 percent are already saving for retirement, and "a significant 21 percent…had a savings account before the age of 10!" Some "77 percent of Gen Z currently earns their own spending money through freelance work, a part-time job, or earned allowance."[32] As one expert contends of this inventive tribe, "Gen Z's practical and fiscally conservative behavior is already making them part of businesses and our economy, despite their young age."[33]

As more and more Gen Zers reach adulthood in the coming years, this expectation-busting behavior is only going to continue. And it is going to shape our world. Keep in mind that in 2019, Gen Z accounted for 32 percent of the world's 7.7 billion people.[34] They number about 90 million in the United States, which is more than ten million more than either the baby boomers or the millennials.[35] Though much attention has focused on the millennials of late, it is Generation Z who will define a considerable portion of the future.

THE BATTLE PLAN

This, then, is the exciting, talented, but troubled generation we now have before us. How do we love them? How do we reach them? How do we battle for them as the warrior generation we are called to be? Allow me to offer a battle plan.

First, we are going to have to awaken a generation of warrior moms. I know this may sound like a contradiction of what I've repeatedly said about our plague of fatherlessness and the importance of men in young lives. Still, it is true, and excellent warriors pay attention to the military intelligence they need wherever it may take them.

The simple truth is that Generation Z is a tribe turned to their mothers. This may be, in part, a function of absentee fathers or the cultural war on men we discussed in chapter 4, but it is a statistically verified truth nevertheless. Gen Zers lean on their mothers, listen to their mothers, rely on their mothers for guidance, seek to please their mothers, and look to their mothers for the relational warmth that centers them and fills their souls.

A recent Barna survey, called the *Households of Faith* report, was conducted in cooperation with Lutheran Hour Ministries. Its findings were stunning. While we might picture Gen Zers, like most teens, rolling their eyes at their parents, the truth is that this tribe is "very open with and dependent on their mothers." Among those teens surveyed, a vast majority pointed to their mothers as their primary activity partners. Some 85 percent eat meals mainly with their mothers, 81 percent watch TV mostly with their mothers, 70 percent talk about God with their mothers, and 63 percent said they have meaningful confrontations with their mothers.[36]

Even more revealing is that the teens surveyed look to their mothers for "advice (78%), encouragement (75%) and sympathy (72%)." Fathers certainly aren't excluded, but the teens said they are most likely to go to their dads for money (74 percent) and logistical help (63 percent).[37]

A critical truth for our efforts to stand guard over this generation is that mothers are the ones who provide spiritual guidance and do the most to shape values and disciplines of faith in Gen Zers. For this young generation, moms are the main prayer partners (63 percent), the chief molders of perceptions of the Bible (71 percent), and the primary sources of answers to faith questions of any kind (72 percent). Mothers are also the ones who encourage church attendance (79 percent), teach about God's forgiveness (66 percent), and impart knowledge about religious traditions (72 percent).[38]

In conclusion of this seminal study, Alyce Youngblood, Barna's managing editor for the *Households of Faith* report, said, "Over and over, this study speaks to the enduring impact of mothers—in conversation, companionship, discipline and, importantly, spiritual development."[39]

I have to say that the use of the words *enduring impact* brings to mind so much throughout history that emphasizes the influential role of mothers. Did you know that the word *mother* is used around three hundred times in the Bible? Did you know that the Hebrew word *mother* in the Old Testament indicates "an intimate relationship" with one "who bestows benefits on others"?[40] Do you remember that Solomon admonished us, "Do not forsake your mother's teaching"?[41] It is also interesting that Jesus addressed one of His seven statements from the cross to His mother.[42] Even while dying, He thought of her and cared for her needs in honor of all she had done for Him.

In addition, I have always been moved by a truth I once learned about men at war. Having lived in rural Pennsylvania and now in Virginia, the Civil War looms large in my mind and imagination. One of the most touching things I know about that war is that dying soldiers spoke one word more than any other. In their last moments, it was the word *mother* that most often came to their lips. They would cry out for their mothers. They would ask friends to pass messages to their mothers. They would weep and ask their mothers to come to them. Always, though, it was their mothers who were on their minds as they stepped into eternity.[43]

The good news for our day is that whatever stresses and strains and nontraditional opinions Generation Z display, they love their mothers and look to them as guides. If we combine this with what we know about the primacy of relationships, about brain science, and about the loneliness and neediness of Generation Z, we can see that godly mothers are the key to protecting and shaping this gifted but challenged generation.

We need warrior moms who see their mothering roles as God-ordained. We need warrior moms who pray for their children and step forcefully and lovingly into their lives. And we need warrior moms who understand, as Psalm 127 has taught us, that they are firing the next generation like arrows into their destiny. All this is true because it is mothers who will most stand guard over this rising generation.

Having said this about the importance of mothers, I also need to emphasize something that will sound strange at first. Particularly because mothers are so critical to shaping Generation Z, they must hear the warning that they can love their children too much. You've probably heard the term *helicopter parents* that was coined in 1989 to refer to the hovering, overprotective parenting style that has become prevalent in recent decades. Sounds ominous, doesn't it? Well, along with Dr. Gary Sibcy, I once wrote an entire book entitled *Loving Your Child Too Much*. I want to add some of the insights from this book to this battle plan for the next generation.

Parents face three primary issues that fall under the umbrella of potentially loving your child too much: overcontrolling, overprotecting, and overindulging. Overprotecting is about safety, overcontrolling is about limits, and overindulging is about a sense of being loved.

I believe that a lot of Christian parents are getting it right. They do an outstanding job of wanting to have some boundaries for their kids. They want them to be safe, and they want them to be loved. The problem is when we get off balance by providing only the love and direction that feel good and shirking the hard work of difficult conversations and loving discipline.

If we don't teach our children a work ethic or if we're always running in and rescuing them, it has an adverse effect on them. Sometimes this comes from within our own needs: "I didn't have anything, so I'm going to give my kids anything they want. Nobody stuck up for me, so I'm going to fight for my kids. I'm terrified of life, so I'm going to stand between my children and any painful thing that might come their way."

The problem is that raising kids this way creates irresponsible people who lack self-sufficiency. They are afraid to take risks, and more, they are overly dependent. I can tell you that the central theme of our book about parents loving their kids too much is that parents often overcompensate because of something lacking in their own lives. They feel like they are loving their kids but are in fact leading them into distance and rebellion.

What can really hurt our kids are neglect, emotional and physical and sexual abuse, unmet emotional needs, control that prevents them from having a voice or identity (placing rules above relationship), a lack of blessing over their lives, and lack of affirmation. We need to support and champion parents in a way that builds emotionally healthy individuals who can then parent from a secure place.

Dr. Dobson years ago said that busy, stressed-out parents are exhausted. When you are overly exhausted, you get grouchy. When you are grouchy, it leads to isolation, and so people move away from you.[44] I agree with Dr. Dobson here, and I remind you that this dynamic includes your kids. As well-known pastor Chuck Swindoll wrote, "The busy, insensitive, preoccupied parent, steamrolling through the day, misses many a cue and sails right past choice moments never to be repeated."[45]

If you are going to raise the next generation of leaders, you need to parent with love and limits. It's okay to tell your kids no. We have to be able to say, "No playing in the street! It's dangerous!" This is, after all, what God does. He tells us not to do the abominable thing that He hates. He says, "Thou shalt not." God, as our perfect, loving Father, gives us limits. Similarly, boundaries with our kids are important—and they take work.

The Bible says, "Train up a child in the way he should go."[46] The literal Hebrew here is "according to his way,"[47] referring to the child's bent. It's an image taken from making bows from tree branches. Each tree limb has a natural bent, so we have to make the bow with an awareness of the tree branch's natural direction and tendencies. It is the same with children. We are to train them in the ways of the Lord while being sensitive to the unique, natural bent the Lord gave each of them.[48]

> You have to catch your kids doing good and learn to reinforce it, to point them toward the good you want to see accomplished in their lives. #focusonthefuture

We must do this, though, while also aware of the truth that "foolishness is bound in the heart of a child; but the rod of correction shall drive it far from him."[49] Grace Ketterman, MD, once told me that "the ever-present shepherd's rod" was "used to prod the wayward sheep away from danger."[50] By this, she meant that the shepherd's staff is about guiding and directing but not beating. So we do need to use the "rod of correction," but it is not a rod for punishment. It is a shepherd's rod for guiding, directing, and making secure through authority.

We fulfill much of this challenge by reinforcing the good. You have to catch your kids doing good and learn to reinforce it, to point them toward the good you want to see accomplished in their lives. We have to pay attention to the old saying "Success begets success." We need to teach our kids to recognize success and head in that positive direction.

The good news is that we love our children and want the best for them. Yet trouble comes into their lives when we don't use godly wisdom mixed with love. If we pamper them, if we insulate them from challenges, if we overwhelm them with gifts without requiring character and good behavior in return, then we will be fashioning self-centered, materialistic, ungrateful, and morally confused children. We can do better than this. God has given us the wisdom of His Word and His Spirit to raise noble children ready to contend with the challenges of their generation.

Finally, in loving and nurturing Generation Z, we are going to have to be skilled in a specific kind of spiritual warfare. We see this described in 2 Corinthians 10:

> The weapons we fight with are not the weapons of the world. On the contrary, they have divine power to demolish strongholds. We demolish arguments and every pretension that sets itself up against the knowledge of God, and we take captive every thought to make it obedient to Christ.
>
> —2 CORINTHIANS 10:4–5

Our beloved Generation Z has a unique way of thinking. They are an intelligent and gifted generation, yet they tend to personalize the experiences of others that they learn about in the news or on the internet in such a way that it causes them deep turmoil and pain. This sets up defense mechanisms against the truth in their minds, defenses that we will have to remove lovingly to help them see the reality of Christ.

For example, it is common knowledge among Christian

counselors who work with Gen Zers that they will often speak of what the church has done to them. When these counselors drill down into what the exact experience of these individuals has been, they often find that nothing has happened personally but that their counselees have absorbed offense from news reports and stories circulating on the internet.

One counselor reported that a young man felt the church had wronged him, even abused him. When the counselor pressed for details, it turned out that the young man had taken up offense for the plague of sexual abuse in the Catholic Church of recent years. The young man spoke as though these wrongs had happened to him, though they hadn't. Now, this abuse was horrible, and all of us ought to feel compassion and pray continually for the healing of the victims. However, there is a difference between caring about a wrong that happened to someone else and living as though it happened to you. Generation Z allows their deep compassion to carry them to the extreme of personalizing trauma that is not truly theirs. This forms itself into an intellectual opposition to wisdom and truth, even resistance to relationships with good and godly people.

When we add to this that Gen Z has been educated in secular and sometimes deeply anti-Christian schools, we see the problem. Formed in their minds are, in the words of Paul the apostle, "strongholds...arguments and every pretension" that array themselves against the gospel of Jesus and the truth in every area of life.

This means we will have to ask God to give us exactly what Paul described: "weapons." We will need creative ways of speaking truth to Gen Z. We will need an anointing from God that breaks yokes of deception. We will need to be clothed in love, gentleness, wisdom, and power when we speak to them. This kind of grace comes from prayer, from fasting, from study, and from a nearly military devotion to rescuing a generation for the glory of God.

It will not be easy. Our enemy has tied many in Generation Z in a tangled web of knots that will require divine gifts to untangle. Yet do not be afraid—it can be done! We should feel just as Mordecai urged Queen Esther to feel—that we have come to this moment "for such a time as this."[51]

CHAPTER 7

EXTERMINATING THE FAITH

I N THE PREVIOUS chapter, we explored our calling to invest
in the next generation. This heartfelt mission, this feeling of
duty, moves me every time I think about it because it is one
of the most powerful forces for good in the history of the world.
Throughout the centuries, courageous souls have done mighty
things out of their belief that they had an obligation to the next
generation. We all want to launch the young to greatness. We
all want to make life better for those who come after us. So, we
work. We sacrifice. We invest in those yet to come. As a result,
immense progress has occurred in the world, and legacies have
developed to lift up generations to come.

It is a biblical concept. Families tend to reproduce themselves
through generations. In my line of work, counselors call this
generational flow and transmission. This can happen with the
good, the bad, and the ugly dynamics and patterns—everything
from explosive anger to church attendance habits. Scripture even
says, "You shall not bow down to them or worship them; for I,
the LORD your God, am a jealous God, punishing the children
for the sin of the parents to the third and fourth generation of
those who hate me."[1] Here's the good news: the Bible goes on

to say, "…but showing love to a thousand generations of those who love me and keep my commandments."[2] This is also why the Genesis 49 passage where Jacob blesses his sons becomes more and more significant to me as a father and grandfather. In his last act as patriarch, he called his sons together for a blessing—and his specific words over his sons played out throughout generations in Scripture. The prophecy spoken in these verses includes reference to Christ's birth many centuries later.

When I think of this dynamic in human affairs, I often think of the 1998 movie *Saving Private Ryan*. Tom Hanks plays Captain John Miller, a man leading his squad through D-Day and into France during some of the fiercest fighting of World War II. His mission is to find Private James Francis Ryan, whose three brothers have died in battle. To prevent the Ryan family from losing all its sons in the war, General George Marshall has ordered that Private Ryan be found and sent home.

Miller leads his seven men through the hell that is war to find Ryan. Some of his men die along the way. All are scarred by what they undergo. Finally, they are forced to join in the battle for control of a bridge at Ramelle. The fighting is fierce. Captain Miller is mortally wounded. Before he dies, he looks Private Ryan firmly in the face and says, "Earn this."

These words capture what every generation hopes the next generation will do:

- Recognize the investment made in them

- Earn what has been sacrificed by those who went before

- Live nobler and loftier lives because of what has been given to them and continue to push forward for those still to come

This is the heartbeat underneath the statistics and stories I have shared in these pages.

We sacrifice so generations to come can thrive and achieve. On the flip side of the coin, we hope to be remembered as significant. We live in the hope that future generations will celebrate our accomplishments. We want to be known as the builders of a firm foundation, remembered by our descendants as honorable and courageous and just.

I can't help but recall some of the great speeches that have captured this soul longing, the powerful words spoken at dramatic moments to inspire a people on to greatness, all by urging them to think about how future generations will remember them.

Winston Churchill, of course, is a great modern example of this. He regularly called the British people and the whole Western world to keep in mind what future generations would think if those living through World War II conducted themselves honorably. For example, on June 18, 1940, he said, "Let us therefore brace ourselves to our duties, and so bear ourselves that, if the British Empire and its Commonwealth last for a thousand years, men will still say, 'This was their finest hour.'"[3]

There is a way of living, then, that is heroic and stalwart and righteous because a people think about how future generations will recall them. They are virtuous and sacrificing because they want to live in a way that future generations will remember with pride.

OUR PRESENT MOMENT

I tell you with all urgency that we live at such a time now. We face significant challenges and threats to the way we are called to live. We must conduct ourselves heroically so that future generations think of this moment as our "finest hour," so that they celebrate our devotion as having saved a godly way of life for their time.

The truth is that for those of us who live for Jesus, who dare to call ourselves Christians in this largely anti-Christian age, there is now an urgent calling on us to be heroes, to contend for the faith and live it nobly so that Jesus is glorified and we pass a holy way of life on to generations yet unborn.

Our times now force us to be courageous. They demand of God's people radical holiness. They require that we live boldly as Christians in the face of the darkness that surrounds us.

I cannot overstate the importance of being a generation that courageously fights for faith and freedom. In their *World Watch List 2020*, Open Doors, the stellar organization founded by Brother Andrew, announced that within their reporting period 2,983 Christians worldwide had been killed for their faith, 3,711 believers had been detained and imprisoned without trial, and 9,488 churches or Christian buildings had been attacked because of the people's devotion to Jesus Christ.[4]

When you let the reality of the individual human lives behind these numbers sink in, you cannot help but be shaken. These statistics are horrible and should sound a trumpet call in our lives. Yet allow me to describe the suffering of women in the world to paint our current crisis in even more personal terms. Every day— think of it, every single day we live in this world—six Christian women are "raped, sexually harassed or forced to marry under threat of execution due to their faith." An early 2018 report documented more than 2,200 such incidents. Tens of millions of Christian women around the world suffer a kind of "double persecution." In many cultures, they are thought to be weak and second-class because of their gender. Then, in addition, they are mistreated because they are Christians.[5] We may have recently experienced a #MeToo moment in the United States, but no such movement toward equality and freedom from abuse is happening for most Christian women in the rest of the world. It is all part of the rising trend of persecution of Christians in our time.

This is currently the state of things outside the United States, and it appears to be only getting worse. The situation is somewhat better in the United States but only because people are not dying in large numbers for their faith in Jesus. Instead, the persecution here is cultural and legal. In a nation founded on Christian principles and purposes, we are now experiencing systematic opposition to the Christian gospel and Christian people in this country. Our Lord is mocked in popular media. Our churches are embattled. The nation's schools virtually ban Christianity and neglect no opportunity to ridicule our faith and to attempt to expose it as a lie. Our families are under siege, and in some parts of the world, our lives and livelihoods are in danger if we profess faith in Jesus Christ.

THE STORIES THAT TELL THE TALE

Let me remind you of a few recent stories from our national headlines to confirm what I am saying. In a famous, disturbing case, Jack Phillips, the Christian owner of a bakery in Lakewood, Colorado, kindly told a gay couple that his Christian convictions prevented him from baking a cake for their same-sex wedding. Other bakeries in town could serve them, and as he explained in a follow-up call, the state of Colorado did not at that time recognize same-sex marriages.

You would think that would be the end of it. Not true. Instead, the gay couple filed a complaint with the Colorado Civil Rights Commission. This complaint led to a lawsuit, *Craig v. Masterpiece Cakeshop*. The cause of the gay couple won in this suit. Jack Phillips was ordered not only to provide wedding cakes for same-sex marriages but also to change his company's policies and offer staff training on the state's nondiscrimination laws. He was also ordered to submit quarterly reports for the following two years to confirm the bakery had complied.

Mr. Phillips appealed. The case worked itself through the court system until it reached the US Supreme Court under the name *Masterpiece Cakeshop, Ltd. v. Colorado Civil Rights Commission*. It was a national sensation, with almost one hundred amicus ("friend of the court") briefs filed in support of one side or the other. Fortunately, the Court ruled in Masterpiece Cakeshop's favor, stating that though Mr. Phillips was a baker, "in his capacity as the owner of a business serving the public," he maintained "his right to the free exercise of religion limited by generally applicable laws."[6]

It would have been bad enough had the matter ended there. That a Christian business owner had been forced to appeal to the nation's highest court just to maintain his fundamental right of free speech is outrage enough. But the whole affair continued. In what was surely an act designed to set up further legal action, in 2017, on the same day the Supreme Court agreed to hear Phillips's case, a woman asked Masterpiece Cakeshop to bake a cake celebrating her gender transition. Phillips, of course, said no, and the lawsuits continue to this day.

Imagine the cost to Mr. Phillips, both in lost business and in legal fees. Imagine the bombardment he has endured. Yet keep in mind that it is all because Jack Phillips is a Christian who wishes to honor God in how he runs his bakery. Such is the state of opposition against Christian people today.

It doesn't end there. Let's consider for a moment the matter of prayer offered before football games at Bradley Central High School in Bradley County, Tennessee. The practice had long been a tradition, as it has been in many other school districts around the United States. Before games, a student would lead a prayer over the sound system. In one such prayer, the student asked God for "safety and great sportsmanship."

In January 2018, though, an anonymous person complained about the prayer and contacted the Freedom From Religion Foundation (FFRF), an organization that seeks to expel any vestige of religion from American public life. The FFRF contacted the school district, complaining that the prayer violated the Constitution and recent US Supreme Court decisions.[7]

Now, we've heard this language so much that it barely pricks our ears. Yet consider for a moment that the basis of the complaint is that the US Constitution, which was written and adopted into law mainly by Christian people, now bans Christian expression at a high school football game.

The legal tug-of-war over this matter of prayer in public school settings continues. What moves me is that, soon after the controversy arose at Bradley Central, the students held an all-volunteer prayer meeting at the football stadium. Thank God for their courage, but if antireligious groups continue to press the matter, both prayer before football games and even student-led all-volunteer prayer meetings in a public school facility could be banned. Such is the state of the law and the anti-Christian bias in our courts and our culture today.

OUR ANTI-CHRISTIAN SOCIETY

Beyond these disturbing legal matters, a broader bias against Christians in American culture increasingly rears its ugly head. The truth is that Christians today often feel frozen out of doing the good they wish to do in a country they love. The reason? There is resistance to their influence in nearly every arena of American life. Some call it cancel culture.

In 2016, the tremendously informative Barna organization conducted a poll of people of faith to understand how they feel about their role in American society. The results were disturbing. Though the vast majority (88 percent) of those surveyed feel that their faith is a force for good in society and 93 percent even believe their faith is essential to society, it is also true that most of these Christians feel opposed in the very society they wish to help. Some 54 percent say they feel misunderstood, and 52 percent say they feel persecuted. Many also say they feel "marginalized" (44 percent), "sidelined" (40 percent), "silenced" (38 percent), "afraid to speak up" (31 percent), and "afraid to look stupid" (23 percent).[8]

Let's take the public schools in the United States as an example. There is little question that public education in this country is in trouble. We regularly hear not only of violence in our schools but also of poor academic performance. The United States continues to show little to no improvement on most lists of educational achievement among nations of the world.[9]

Americans know this and find it disturbing. In a 2014 Barna study, only 7 percent of adults in this country said they believe that the nation's public schools are "very effective." Almost half, some 46 percent, were sure that public schools had further declined in the previous five years. Moreover, among parents of school-age children, only one-third (34 percent) said that public education is the first choice for their children.[10]

The situation is dire, and Christians would like to make a difference. Why? Because 34 percent believe that improving public education is vital to demonstrating Christian concern for their communities, and 33 percent think that helping the public schools is part of helping the poor and the needy. For these and other reasons, 95 percent of all Protestant pastors believe that Christians should be involved in helping America's public schools, and more than 80 percent of churchgoing Christians agree.[11] Many of these understand that local congregations already contribute to the educational levels of their communities, and they would like to do more.

Yet many Christians feel unwelcomed by the very schools they would like to help. About 18 percent of the Christians surveyed reported that they don't think public schools want the help of religious people. Another 18 percent believe that public education is "too political" and not in the direction a traditional Christian would fit. About 9 percent believe that "public school culture is contrary to religious beliefs," and thus Christians are not welcome. More practically, 17 percent are unsure of how to help.[12]

The tragedy, then, is that Christians who care about their communities and are already raising educational levels through their local churches feel that their help is not wanted in public schools. They see public education as an arena hostile to their faith, one that is highly political and turned against traditional values and faith. The recent debate on critical race theory and the endorsement of this position by the National Education Association (NEA) only creates even greater suspicion and intense concern for parents over what's being taught in their children's schools.

So even though Christians are doing their best to help, they feel public school culture is antagonistic to them and opposed to much that they believe. This too is a form of persecution, and it is felt in many arenas of our national life. There is a rising bias against Christian believers throughout our nation today.

OUR INVISIBLE ENEMY

Look at the sentence that ends the previous paragraph: "There is a rising bias against Christian believers throughout our nation today." That dynamic is one of the most important trends shaping American life today. Yet I would not be surprised if you had to think twice about the anti-Christian bias you've experienced. It's not always obvious, is it? It usually isn't overt.

Now, if you are like me and you read of the kind of anti-Christian bigotry I've described above, you are ready to storm your local PTA meeting or even the gates of hell, if need be. You are stirred up and eager to go out in the streets and stand heroically against the evils of our age. I wish it were that visceral, that physical, and that simple. It isn't.

Instead, the enemies in our age aren't arrayed on physical battlefields, easy to see and easy to target. No, they are invisible. They are spiritual. They are intellectual. And they are sneaky.

To put this in terms of military theory, our enemies today aren't conventional forces. They don't line up in brightly colored uniforms, ten thousand strong, and dare us to come out to battle. Instead, our enemies today, both visible and invisible, fight as guerrilla forces. They probe for weakness, avoid confrontation, and sneak around to unguarded places. They hit where we least expect it. In a word, they don't play fair.

You may remember studying in high school history class the time when this type of warfare began to gain the upper hand. Do you remember learning about how our colonial American minutemen fought against the British troops at the start of the American Revolution? The British fought conventionally, in bright red uniforms and massive formations. They lined up openly on battlefields, having marched for miles, all while making a tremendous amount of noise and announcing their presence brashly.

The minutemen, though, had learned battle tactics from Native Americans. They moved stealthily through the forest. They wore their own clothes instead of uniforms. They did not fight openly in large numbers but fired on the British from hiding places, a few men at a time shooting at just the right moment. They wore the British down. They dispirited them. The minutemen were hard to see, hard to fight, hard to kill, and hard to capture. The

British officers wrote back to England of their complete frustration with this new kind of warfare.

It is the same for us today. We might do better if our opponents lined up openly and announced their intentions. They don't. They fight as guerrilla forces do. For example, we would probably prefer if the forces of secularism argued with us about the existence of Jesus and the historical truth of the Bible. We might do better in battle. Our pastors are taught how to answer these challenges in their seminaries. We can handle this kind of fight.

Yet what happens today is that our critics work to repackage Christianity. We believers in Jesus think that we are devoted to loving people and trying to do good in the world. In our hearts we hold tenaciously to the Golden Rule. But opponents of Christianity today have learned to present our faith in different ways, including as something dark and misguided. They want to portray Christians as anything but loving and kind in how we're living out our faith life. Even more than outdated, we are supposedly filled with hate and an actual danger to civilization. You've heard the charges or seen them posted on social media. According to some, the Christian community is outdated, ill-informed, intolerant, haters, anti-LGBTQ bigots, and racists. We oppose all other faiths, and we are trying to gain the controls of government to force our faith on others, much like the Nazis of the last century; they are broad-stroking some as Christian nationalists or insurrectionists.

Suddenly, instead of having to answer for telling people God loves them, caring for their practical needs, or encouraging healthy, loving families, those who love God and appreciate their freedom are painted as the enemies of society, a cancer that will destroy American democracy. For evidence, we have only to look at the use of the word *evangelical* today. Modern media practically uses it as a synonym for a disease or a terrorist movement.

The truth is, though, that the term refers to those who believe in "good news." (In the original Greek language of the Bible, the term *euangélion* means "good news.")[13]

SILENCED, STIGMATIZED, SHAMED

I've mentioned the media, so allow me to stay on this subject before I start talking about solutions. In my field of mental health, we often use three *S* words to describe how people shut each other down. They *silence* them, they *stigmatize* them, and they *shame* them—a perfect description of what is happening to Christians in modern American society.

First, Christians are systematically denied avenues to share our message, from manger scenes to open profession of our faith in the public arena, from public prayer to schoolteachers daring to keep a Bible on their desks. In other words, Christian people are being silenced in America today. We all know it. The stories fill the headlines nearly every day.

Then, believers in Jesus are stigmatized. You've seen this in television shows and movies, in literature and popular comedy: the religious people are the weirdos; the Christian pastor in a police drama is often the pervert or the criminal. The natural conclusion is that religion is a sickness, faith is toxic. It's painted as a pathology. In this way, Christians and their gospel are stigmatized.

Finally, they are shamed. What? You don't want a transgender person reading stories to your child at the public library? Shame on you. How unloving you are! How cold-hearted! And you say you don't want your five-year-old to determine his gender for himself? How unenlightened you must be! What a hindrance to the progress of society your faith is! And so it goes. You see it, and you know it for what it is: the new progressivism.

> The political Left in America has become the
> champion of a new, secular, anti-Christian political
> religion that is as intolerant as any faith that has
> ever stalked the earth. #focusonthefuture

I have to speak bluntly about this. The radical political Left in America has become the champion of a new, secular, anti-Christian political religion that is as intolerant as any faith that has ever stalked the earth. Just consider what has happened to America in the matter of lifestyles. A visitor from Mars might assume the United States makes all its decisions based on what sexual practices an individual chooses. This is because if the Left had its way, we would select judges, presidents, pastors, professors, police officers, ambassadors, and all other officials in society based pretty exclusively on their sexual views and practices. This goes on while our elites eschew and condemn Christianity, despite research supporting that the tenets of our faith practices are healthy and life-giving. We've seen many of them in the pages of this book.

SOLUTIONS FOR OUR AGE

So let's start talking about solutions.

To state it bluntly, now is a time for fierce courage. The spirit of our age works to make us cowards, to fill us with moral compromise and doubts about the truth of God. Fear makes you play small. Timid. This same spirit strives to make us retreating and inconsequential, feeling like there is nothing we can do in the face of such threatening and fierce opposition.

Hear me: it is a lie! It is a deception. The truth is that people devoted to Jesus are powerfully armed with the gospel and weapons capable of rescuing souls and changing our generation. Now is the time to reclaim confidence in who God is, in who we are, and in the gifts God has given us. Now is the time—I say it again—for courage.

Let me stay on this important theme for a moment. We must be courageous, most of all, because God commands it. The Bible tells us, "Be strong and courageous. Do not be afraid or terrified because of them, for the LORD your God goes with you; he will never leave you nor forsake you."[14] We are meant not just to show courage at certain moments but to live courageous lives. Let me state it firmly: We are not in this world for pleasure. We are not here merely to build self-satisfied lives. Instead, we are here to live godly lives, proclaim godly truth in love, and send forth in the world a godly young generation. It means we must face our fears and any dangers before us. We must have courage, of a kind fueled by God's Spirit, to do this.

Second, courage is a trait that most reveals who God is to the world. We do not win the hearts of non-Christian people by being weak and fearful. We do not impress by retreating or hiding away. Instead, courage makes an impression and shows that we are a people connected to a real and living God. The Bible says as much. The apostle Paul tells us to live "without being frightened in any way by those who oppose you. This is a sign to them that they will be destroyed, but that you will be saved—and that by God."[15] In short, courage convinces. Courage reveals. Courage makes the case that our God is real and that we will not flinch or retreat because He is in our lives.

Third, courage is the force that most clearly reveals that we have Christ in us. I know you believe as I do that Christ-filled people ought to be different. They ought to stand out, not fit in. People ought to look at them and say, "These folks have something supernatural in their lives, a bold love for God and others, and in that order."

In an age when fear abounds and people are desperately

looking about for anyone who can point the way, the courage of Christian people will cause nonbelievers to look at us with respect and make them willing to hear what we have to say. Not because we have pretty church buildings or wear stylish clothes. Not because we have good music or put on entertaining events. No! Because we stand fearless in the face of the torments of our time, anchored in love and ever pointing to Jesus Christ as the source of all life. This will win the doubting and draw the terrified.

Finally, our entire message of the cross is made real by our courage. Think about it. We call people to believe what Jesus did on the cross, to embrace that cross, and to take up their own crosses daily. This isn't just meaningless religious rhetoric. The cross was a means of execution. It's like saying today, "Let Christians take up their electric chairs every day." That's how powerful it is. Well, if we really believe this, if we confront death every day, then courage should be the result. We don't fear death. We don't fear those who can only kill the body. We don't fear persecution. We are as courageous as our God calls us to be because we have died to self and live for the cross of Jesus. This determination is what makes our message real to a dying world.

I want what was said of the apostles in the first century to be said of you and me. After Jesus had been crucified and raised from the dead, Peter and John were preaching the gospel. The Bible gives us a glimpse into what the religious leaders of the day thought about these men. Watch the words here carefully: "When they saw the courage of Peter and John and realized that they were unschooled, ordinary men, they were astonished and they took note that these men had been with Jesus."[16]

Notice, they saw Peter and John's courage first and foremost. Then they realized that what these men had was not produced by extensive education. Instead, the religious leaders were astonished to realize that it was a result of having spent so much time with Jesus.

This is what we want today. They see our courage, always anchored in God's love. They see the imprint of Jesus on our lives. They are astonished. Eventually, they follow us as we follow Jesus. It all starts with courage. It all begins with an impressive boldness that we desperately need today.

We must be both courageous and passionately biblical. I know this must sound obvious since I am a Christian writer focused mainly on Christians in this book. Yet not only do the statistics reveal that we have a crisis of biblical illiteracy in our time, but the challenges of our age also force us to be distinctly biblical if we are going to be victorious in what we are called to do.

The statistics are convicting. According to a survey done by Lifeway Research, 87 percent of households in this country own a Bible. That's pretty astonishing for a country that many experts call "post-Christian." But it is also true that only 20 percent of Americans have read the Bible all the way through, and 53 percent of all Americans have read only a few scattered passages.[17]

Yet the problem isn't what happens in society but what happens in our homes and the church. As we might expect, evangelicals are more likely to read a bit of the Bible every day. However, this is true only of half of all evangelicals. Among non-evangelicals, only 16 percent read the Bible daily. And 36 percent of Protestants read Scripture every day, compared with 17 percent of Catholics.

So, in short, even Christians are not feeding on the spiritual diet God intends for His people. This means that we do not have the necessary knowledge to counter the flood of information coming our way from our increasingly secular society.

I can support this statement very simply. Think for a moment about how much time you spend reading Scripture. Now, think

146

about how much time you spend watching television. Point made. We are living in a kind of battle of information today, and if we do not counter with Scripture the worldly information that floods into our lives, we are going to be shaped by this age and its values. Remember, the Bible tells us, "Do not conform to the pattern of this world, but be transformed by the renewing of your mind."[18]

> The problem we deal with today is not just that some refuse to believe our faith; it is that they dare to rewrite our faith or remake it in the image of society. #focusonthefuture

We need to center on the Bible to know biblical truth that can counter the distortions of our age. I've often heard this thought: The great Christian fear of our time is not so much that society rejects the gospel. It is that society is successful in rewriting the gospel. I agree with this. The problem we deal with today is not just that some refuse to believe our faith; it is that they dare to rewrite our faith or remake it in the image of society. You see this all the time. How many people now say that an LGBTQ agenda is consistent with Scripture? How many people now see Jesus Christ as almost a New Age guru rather than who He really was? How many now compromise with the world on abortion or drunkenness or horoscopes, all while citing Scripture in support for what they do?

We have to know our faith so we can give an answer. We have to be ready to expose these lies and bring every thought captive to the obedience of Christ, as the apostle Paul tells us so powerfully. Our ignorance of biblical teaching only allows a fallen society to chip away at the edifice of our faith.

Yet beyond all these reasons for making the Bible central to our lives, one of the most important is that the Bible brings us spiritual power to live in this age. You see, the Scriptures are not just natural words of information. They are Spirit-filled. Jesus said, "The words I have spoken to you—they are full of the Spirit and life."[19] When we read the Scriptures, memorize them, and meditate on them, they deposit spiritual power in our lives.

I've heard Christian teachers urge us to think of the sentences in the Bible as little trains, with each word being a train car that deposits Spirit and life into our hearts. It is a helpful image, and if we take the Scriptures in, then we will receive not only information but also the power behind the information that can transform us and equip us to live in this age.

RECLAIMING THE FAMILY

To face the age of challenge and persecution we are living in, we need to be courageous, and we need to be anchored biblically. Yet I also want to urge us to do something that should be no surprise if you've been with me through all that I've said in this book so far. I want to urge us to strengthen the family.

The simple truth is that much of the opposition to our faith today takes the form of opposition to the family—and our families, as we've seen, are not in great shape in our generation. Just consider for a moment the way the family is targeted in most central issues today.

What is abortion but an assault on the lives of babies and the God-given role of motherhood? Abortion targets the next generation and is a denial of the priority of family life. What is the loss of masculinity but a damaging of family and children and a devaluing of the legacy for future generations? What is the radical LGBTQ agenda except a complete upheaval of the God-given role of men and women and His design for the family? What is the rise of the nanny state other than a replacement of family authority with governmental demands and programs? In all of these the family is deeply affected.

Let me take this point further. If an evil force sat in a conference room and tried to decide how to uproot Christianity from a society it wanted to dominate, it could do no better than to attack the family. It would destroy men. It would work to diminish the awesome power of valiant womanhood. It would redefine the family in a perverse and unbiblical fashion. It would kill the young and usurp parental authority. It would use popular media to portray the traditional family as stifling and deforming and unworkable.

In the days to come, we have to win our generation by offering it examples of dynamic, loving, life-changing families. We have to model what the kingdom of God looks like by modeling godly families that are counter to the spirit of the age. In short, we have to live out what Dr. James Dobson has taught us and what we have been surveying in the pages of this book. We can win the battle for souls in our generation. We can win the battle for winning our nation back to God. Yet we can do it only from a base of powerfully, biblically, spiritually alive churches and loving, honoring, nurturing families devoted to Jesus.

Here's the good news: it can be done! And we can do it. Now is our time. And the righteous church and family are the way we fulfill our mission.

CHAPTER 8

A BRIDE MADE READY

H E WAS A historian, a diplomat, and a pioneering political scientist. He wrote volumes of cultural analysis that are still in print to this day, over two centuries after he was born. He also served his nation as a minister of foreign affairs and as a valued advisor. He was the kind of man who is rare in every age: a wise man, a man of insight, always looking for the truth.

There are many reasons to admire Alexis de Tocqueville, yet chief among them is the prophetic understanding he had of America. When he toured the young United States in 1831, he was deeply impressed by the role of Christianity in the lives of the American people. Such vitality of faith was new to him. He wrote, "I had almost always seen the spirit of religion and the spirit of freedom pursuing courses diametrically opposed to each other; but in America I found they were intimately united, and that they reigned in common over the same country."[1]

He went in search of the meaning of this "spirit of religion" for America. He found that in this new land, religion "must...be regarded as the foremost of the political institutions." He recognized that "in the United States the sovereign authority is religious." He saw that faith was "indispensable to the maintenance of republican institutions."[2]

Imagine it. A Frenchman, fresh from a nation that less than fifty years before had many dechristianized influences during the revolution, finds the true power of America. It is her faith. It is her devotion to God. It is a power that rises from her pulpits on fire with righteousness. This is what has made the nation great. As de Tocqueville wrote, "The Americans combine the notions of Christianity and of liberty so intimately in their minds, that it is impossible to make them conceive the one without the other."[3]

We should take these words and make them our own. We should remember what de Tocqueville found in our country. We should not let the secularists and the textbooks that leave God out of the story and the intimidations of our anti-Christian legal system talk us out of the faith at the foundation of our nation. Nor should we be made to forget or be embarrassed about the role of the churches in our early national life. It mattered to them!

Remember that it was members of a church who sailed to the New World and wrote in the famous Mayflower Compact that they had embarked on their mission "for the glory of God, and advancement of the Christian faith."[4] Remember that it was churches ignited by revival during the Great Awakening that first unified our country and instilled in it a spirit of liberty. And remember that during the American Revolution, the churches were so influential in that mighty struggle that the British army worked hard to capture as many colonial churches as they could and then turn them into riding stables or hospitals or tear them down for firewood.

This was the mighty role of the churches in our nation's founding, and it can be their role again today. We will need renewal, though. We will need a fierce return to every word of Scripture. We will need an end of dead tradition and a willingness to go boldly into our cities and our countrysides to proclaim the power of the gospel of Jesus.

De Tocqueville's words live in my heart. Yet they stand alongside other equally prophetic words that have lived just as powerfully in my heart. Years ago, I was attending a roundtable event, and we were just about to pray for our nation. Before we began, though, Dr. Dobson spoke to all in attendance. He said, "We need to pray that the church will awaken and take her rightful place. Until then, parachurch organizations must stand in the gap—but we must pray that the church be awakened."[5]

These words have never left me. I genuinely believe in Christian organizations that are outside the institutional church. Yet Dr. Dobson was right. We should never cease believing that it is the church in this nation—filled with holy passion, pulpits powered by righteousness—that is the answer for the ills of our time. We should never allow ourselves to be talked out of this vision, this hope, and this purpose.

THE BEDFORD BOYS

When I think of not being talked out of our purpose, I inevitably think about a monument near my home in Virginia. When the torrent of World War II was just gaining force, the people of the town of Bedford in the Shenandoah Valley of Virginia knew that it would change their lives forever. Part of the reason for this was that Company A of the 116th Infantry Regiment, 29th Division, was headquartered in Bedford and included thirty-seven of the town's men. So, when this unit was called into action, they moved out and joined the fight.

These men fought bravely and faced many hardships in their part of the war. Yet the worst came on June 6, 1944—D-Day. Shortly after that, the telegrams began to arrive in Bedford. There was one. Then came a few more. They were the notices informing Bedford families of their dead sons, brothers, fathers, and husbands. In all, there were twenty.

In Bedford today, a beautiful monument honors these men and all who lost their lives on D-Day. It opened in June 2001 and was part of the inspiration for the film *Saving Private Ryan*. In fact, Steven Spielberg helped fund the memorial in honor of his father, a World War II veteran.

Now you see why I cannot think of vision, hope, and purpose without thinking of the Bedford Boys and that stunning monument. Those men gave their all. It makes me want to give my all too, to see the church in this nation become all God intended her to be.

FAKE NEWS ABOUT THE CHURCH

I say these things at a time when there is much opposition to the churches in our country. The media delights in reporting that church attendance is dropping in our land. Increasing numbers of Americans call themselves "nones," meaning people who do not check any traditional religious affiliation on a standard form. We also see the young abandon our churches in shocking numbers, and we see some of the same troubling trends of suicide, mental turmoil, and broken homes bedevil our churches in the way these conditions have stricken the broader society. It is enough to tempt us to think that we really do, as some scholars and observers contend, seem to be heading for (or are already in) a post-Christian America.

Let me remind you of this: in God's governing of the world, the church is plan A, and there is no plan B!

Now, since there is so much opposition against the Christian church in our nation today, let me hit some falsehoods head-on. I do this to encourage you and in hopes that by defying the lies coming against us, we will be inspired to rise and fulfill the calling of our Lord in this hour.

> In God's governing of the world, the church is plan A, and there is no plan B! #focusonthefuture

You've probably heard the many predictions of the decline of Christianity in the United States today. Some folks say that America is heading in the same direction as Europe, just fifty years behind. Others even go so far as to say that Christianity is on the road to extinction in this country.

I don't believe it is so! You see, when analysts look for signs of religious decline in our country, they have to look at externals. That's all they can use to determine matters of faith since they can't look inside people's hearts. So, they tally up church attendance numbers or frequency of Bible reading numbers or other such externally visible matters that sometimes signify devotion to religion. They conclude from such statistics that Christianity is in decline.

I contend, though, that what is in decline is nominal Christianity. Some have called it lukewarm Christianity or mere cultural Christianity. You see, many people identify themselves as Christians for purely cultural reasons.[6] On a form, they will put down the religious affiliation of their family, whether they are personally committed to the faith or not. They will sometimes identify themselves with Christianity because it is advantageous to do so. It allies them with the most influential religious institutions in the nation.

This is what many have done in the past. They were nominal Christians, but they publicly listed themselves as Christians, whether they were deeply devoted or not. Now that we live in different religious times, times when Christianity is under attack worldwide, these nominal Christians aren't as eager to publicly identify themselves by faith in Jesus Christ. Christianity may not be as popular among the people they know or where they work. Saying they're Christians may not be as advantageous. So, they stop listing themselves as Christians on the religious sections of questionnaires. If someone asks them outright, they look for other terms to describe themselves. In the words of a modern-day scholar of religious trends, Ed Stetzer, "the nominals are becoming the nones."[7]

This isn't too surprising. To state it in brief, people identify themselves as Christians for one of three primary reasons: (1) They say they are Christians to distinguish themselves from other faiths like Judaism, Islam, Hinduism, and so forth. In other words, they make a cultural distinction by calling themselves Christian, but they aren't necessarily describing spiritual realities. (2) They say they are Christians because they occasionally attend church. We all know folks like this, and we may even joke that they are Easter and Christmas Christians. (3) Then, of course, there are the believers who say they are Christian because they have had a sincere heart conversion that defines them in every aspect of their lives.[8]

When seasons of persecution and opposition come against those who call themselves Christians, the cultural Christians and occasional church attendees drop off. They don't want to wear the label *Christian* when times are hard. So they start listing themselves as nones. I believe the rise of the nones represents the nominal Christians getting honest with themselves—or perhaps shrinking in fear from the angry face of an anti-Christian culture.

THE GOOD NEWS

I'm going to surprise you by telling you that I think this overall trend is a good thing for those of us who are committed to Jesus Christ. As Ed Stetzer says, "Christianity is not collapsing, but it is being clarified."[9]

The truth is that the number of evangelicals in America has remained relatively steady since the early 1970s. These numbers even include the participation in evangelical churches among youth. Yet mainline Protestants have seen a severe decline, and I believe this is where the rising number of nones is coming from— from "Christians" who had a cultural affiliation to faith, not necessarily a conversion-born heart religion.[10]

By contrast, the number of Americans who say they've been born again has remained fairly steady for decades—in the range of 36 percent to 47 percent. And within the born-again-oriented community, Pentecostal/Charismatic denominations such as the Foursquare Church and the Assemblies of God have seen dramatic growth in some districts.[11]

Stetzer summarizes this beautifully: "Even in the shadow of the decline of cultural and nominal religion, the future of vibrant Christianity in America is all around us. The future of Christianity in America is not extinction but clarification that a devout faith is what will last."[12]

To state this in more biblical terms, everything that can be shaken is being shaken. It may even be that judgment is beginning in the house of God, as Scripture assures us. The faithful should welcome all of this. All of this should be encouraging.

Rather than a Christian church that is polluted by compromise and filled with uncertain believers, a church is arising in our day and in our nation that will increasingly be passionate, devoted, fiery, and eager to engage the surrounding culture. As this progresses, the Christian presence in America will look like a bride that "has made herself ready."[13] No more will we be a sleeping, compromising church that stirs no souls, makes no disciples, fails to impact culture, and does not know the voice of her Lord and bridegroom.

In short, when you hear predictions of the rise of the nones and the decline of the church, pray for two things. Pray that the process of purifying continues. Then pray for those who have backed away from passionate faith and are willing to drift along in none-ville. These people need to come home. They need to see Jesus and live their lives in the transforming community of devoted Christian people.

Let me give you some more good news: The truth is that the numbers we hear about the nones are fluid. They change. They aren't fixed. And when they change, they often change in the direction of people gravitating back to faith and back into churches.[14]

You see, while the media in our country wants to speak of the nones as though they have firmly decided the direction they are going, the facts just don't support this view. Given what we are learning about the nones, it is probably better to think of them simply as people who are undecided, in transition, or yet to make firm decisions. What the nones are *not* is a firm class of people who are committed to being nones forever.

We should know, first of all, that "switching religion is a common occurrence in the United States."[15] We are a nation of seekers; we are spiritually hungry people in search of answers. So we pursue, we morph, we shift in matters of religion more than almost any other people on earth. According to one survey, for example, between 2010 and 2014, "nearly 1 in 5 Americans changed their faith identity."[16] Think about this! A whopping 20 percent of the nation changed its religious affiliation in just four years. Amazing!

Now, here is some even more intriguing news. According to this same survey and during this same four-year period, 48 percent of agnostics and 42 percent of nones made a change from where they were in 2010 to a whole new faith perspective. This means that nearly half of the agnostics in the US in 2010 were no longer agnostics by 2014. And the trend is almost the same for the nones. An equally fascinating trend is that some 17 percent of nones returned to church between 2010 and 2014.[17]

This confirms that the categories we keep hearing about—nones in particular—are a constantly changing group of people and that nones are really "undecideds" or "folks who are unsure" or even "people seeking more." So I'm not afraid of the numbers we keep hearing about nones, nor do I believe that these statistics confirm some permanent decline for the church. Instead, I believe that God is at work, that people are hungry, that cultural Christianity is proving unsatisfying to the human soul, and that people are seeking more. In short, the nones give us a tremendous opportunity to win people out of cultural religion and into a meaningful, saving, transforming relationship with Jesus Christ. Let's choose to see what the media presents as bad news as instead a great window of opportunity for the people of God!

Again, I don't believe the statistics we hear about the nones are a sign of permanent decline for the Christian faith. What I do believe is that God is shaking us, ridding us of lukewarm and merely cultural Christianity, and getting us ready for His purposes. He's awakening His church and preparing us for the future. This is what I want to focus on here. To do so, I want to start with a story from American history.

WHAT SHAKING PRODUCES

Pretty much everyone over college age remembers where he or she was and what he or she was doing on September 11, 2001. People were terrified—fear shot through our nation. Uncertainty ruled the day. In response, people flooded into the nation's churches. Do you remember this? The headlines were filled with reports of this shocking occurrence. People who had not been to church in years were sitting in a church the very next Sunday morning after that horrible day of destruction and bloodshed.

What is the lesson of that time? When world events overwhelm people's souls, they turn to God. They turn to church. They seek help in the arms of the Christian community and the Savior Christians proclaim.

Yet 9/11 wasn't the first time this happened. Let me tell you a story from even earlier in American history. When our nation was just decades old, a series of earthquakes struck the entire Central Mississippi region of the country. This occurred between December 16, 1811, and February 7, 1812. Together these came to be known as the New Madrid Earthquakes, among the most powerful in the history of the United States.

The sheer force of this series of earthquakes was astounding. Trees snapped like twigs by the thousands. Over 800 miles away, President James Madison awoke from a sound sleep in the White House and wondered about the rumbling sound that disturbed his rest.

The quake was so disrupting that the Mississippi River appeared to flow backward for hours, and its course changed permanently. As one historian has written, "Directly across the Mississippi from New Madrid and only a few miles away from the river, near the border of Kentucky and Tennessee, a monstrous section of ground sank as if stepped upon and mashed down by some gigantic foot and water from subterranean sources gushed forth in fantastic volume and quickly filled the huge depression."[18] An entire lake was formed that exists to this day.

Though our history books rarely record it, there was a

significant surge of humanity into churches as a result of these occurrences. As one observer wrote shortly afterward, "It was a time of great terror to sinners."[19] People associated the quakes with the judgment of an angry God, and with each new tremor, hearts shook free of their wickedness. Another observer wrote, "Preachers were everywhere implored to preach and to pray for the people; there was a great awakening among the inhabitants, while men's hearts failed them, and their knees smote together with fear."[20] Denominations grew and planted new churches as sinners were converted. And why? Because the events were too much to face without God, faith, and the security of a vibrant Christian community.

PREPARING OURSELVES

I believe that just as the violent New Madrid earthquakes terrorized people and caused them to flood into churches, we are going to experience much the same in our day. The simple truth is that we are living in times of upheaval. You feel it like I do, I'm sure. You turn on the news and find yourself steeped in the most sickening, upsetting, disorienting stories. It seems that there is no tether, no moral bounding, no vision of good and appropriate— all have been discarded in our age.

Allow your mind to summon the scenes for a moment. Like me, you've probably seen shootings, stabbings, and violent assaults, all while sitting with your family at dinner or trying to rest in your living room. I recently took stock of one evening's headlines. They included not only everything I've listed so far but also stories about parents who conspired to kill their child and nearly overwhelming news about health trends, global warming, political upheaval, and what the economy will mean for the future of our children. It seems as the Bible predicts: "People will faint from terror, apprehensive of what is coming on the world."[21]

The constant pressure of images and headlines like these—not to mention the challenges people are going through in their personal lives beyond what they hear on the news—is causing human hearts to be overwhelmed. People are looking for answers now and will continue to even more desperately in the future. They will increasingly find the tissue-thin answers of our age wanting, and the eternity in their hearts will make them hunger for a connection to God. That's when they'll do what some of them will not have done for decades: turn to the church for the eternal truths that will save them.

Here's my question: Will we be ready? Are our churches able to face the very thing we often pray for—for the lost to flood into our doors seeking salvation? Again I ask, Are we ready?

> As much as I love the church of Jesus Christ in my land, I fear we aren't as ready for what is coming as we ought to be. #focusonthefuture

As much as I love the church of Jesus Christ in my land, I fear we aren't as ready for what is coming as we ought to be. I suspect that our "ships," our churches, may not be equal to the tumultuous waters they will have to traverse in the years to come. We may be too tethered to the current culture, too wedded to dead traditions, too mired in a compromised gospel, and too timid in our biblical distinctives to offer a traumatized society the answer of the kingdom of God. I'm not accusing; I'm just asking a hard question we all must ask ourselves. Are we ready?

If we aren't, we have to get ready. The gospel and the lives it builds are the answers to our sick and terrorized world. I want to say it again: the church is plan A, and there is no plan B. We are going to have to embody the bride who has made herself ready—both for her task and for her bridegroom. The time is now.

THE WAY IT WAS

Allow me to go down memory lane for a moment. I remember that when I was a child, the church was the center of my family's life. We attended a service on Sunday morning after we also attended Sunday school. Then, we attended church on Sunday nights. Was that all until the following week? No. We also attended church on Wednesday night, and I participated in a youth group on Friday night.

Yet our lives were centered on more than just the church meetings. Our lives revolved around God and His truth as we heard it from the pulpit and delved into it in our Bibles. Sitting with other people hearing this truth produced a kind of community and connectivity among the faithful that defined who we were and shaped everything about us.

The Christian community of my youth had a very practical impact on our towns and cities. People seemingly lived more responsible, moral lives because of what the church proclaimed. Christian relationships reinforced a desire to live the highest life we could to honor God and serve each other. Folks were fed, counseled, comforted, guided, taught, restored, and challenged to be their best—all because the church proclaimed and radiated the life, the Word, and the Spirit of the living God.

> I know that Christianity is often marginalized in our society and that Christians have gotten used to it. Let me say loudly that it won't be like that for long. #focusonthefuture

You can see why I dream of the church being that same kind of force today. I know that Christianity is often marginalized in our society and that Christians have gotten used to it. Let me say loudly that it won't be like that for long. I believe the outbreak of COVID-19 and its ensuing economic and cultural reverberations are a foreshadowing of things to come. We're headed for tough times. People will be overwhelmed, they will desperately search for meaning and rescue, and they will start flooding into the churches. At that time, the churches will move from the periphery of our culture to the heart of it, and if we are ready for that moment, we can change the world. We will have the opportunity to make a reality what we have thus far only prayed for and dreamed.

So, let's get practical. What do we have to do to be the bride who has made herself ready? Allow me to list some of the shifts and emphases that I believe we need to invest ourselves in if we are going to be prepared for what is coming.

THE CHANGES WE MUST MAKE

One of the first shifts many churches need to make is to focus on the future. Now I am not just saying this because focusing on the future is the central theme of this book. I'm saying it because it is a matter of survival.

I'm sorry to say it, but many churches in our land are more like museums than they are families of the faithful committed to the radical message of Jesus Christ. It is easy to understand why this is so. Churches tend to come into being because of historical events. This is pretty much as it should be. From a great revival in England under John Wesley, the Methodist Church arose. A movement in the wake of Martin Luther's ministry led to the Lutheran Church. Controversies in church history gave rise to movements defined by certain doctrines. Churches arose as a result.

All this is fine unless these churches define themselves only in terms of their past. Like you, I've been in churches where the artwork, the Sunday sermon, and the passions of the people are all centered on the heroic stands their founders took hundreds of years ago. These can be inspiring memories, but they aren't meant to be the mainstays of these churches today. It leaves these churches looking backward and intent upon refighting battles from generations ago. This leaves them ineffective in the battles of our day. It also means they are missing their "for such a time as this" purpose in the urgent present.

The truth is that it is incredibly easy to fall behind in this generation. Things are changing rapidly. Even if you are trying hard to keep up, the sheer speed of change makes it difficult. Just ponder for a moment the tides of transformation that are sweeping over our age. Do you know that, on average, information doubles in our day just about every thirteen months?[22] Do you know that, as Moore's law says, our technological capability doubles every two years? And consider this: in the Middle Ages, all the knowledge the average person had to know in his or her entire life was equal to the information in one Sunday edition of the *New York Times* today.[23] Think about that compared with what you have to know today just to be an informed citizen of the world.

I say all this to make the point that if you are just standing still, you will find yourself far behind in life because of the rapid change of our times. If you are always looking backward and mentally living in an earlier time, as many of our churches are doing, you will fall behind at a dramatic speed. And like these churches, you will miss your mission, your purpose, and the impact you have been ordained by God to make.

Let me be clear. We don't want our churches to be merely the

Church of What's Happening Now. We don't want churches that are so filled with the philosophies of the current culture and the latest trends and the most stylish ideas that they aren't biblical and have no supernatural power. We aren't trying to be cool and accepted by the guardians of secularism. It does no good to be relevant if it causes us to compromise the truth. We must instead speak the truth in love; we must communicate meaningfully to a culture in crisis. We are trying to lead. All this means we will have to stop being backward focused, stop being museums, and turn instead to ready the churches of Jesus Christ for a challenging but ultimately victorious future.

LOVING ONE ANOTHER

Once we stand firmly in the present with an eye on the future, we are going to have the opportunity to recover a vital truth of biblical Christianity. It is so simple that it would be easy to overlook, but this truth is the key to our impact in the days ahead. It is simply this: we are the church, the people, the believers, the followers of Jesus Christ who can show His love to each other.

I've been emphasizing our human relationships as much as possible in these pages. We've seen how vital our relationships are to our happiness, to healthy brains, to healing trauma, and to raising healthy families. Let me assure you also that our relationships with other believers, second only to the person, will, and work of Jesus Christ Himself, are the most important part of our churches.

Hebrews 13:1–3 sets the vision: "Keep on loving one another as brothers and sisters. Do not forget to show hospitality to strangers, for by so doing some people have shown hospitality to angels without knowing it. Continue to remember those in prison as if you were together with them in prison, and those who are mistreated as if you yourselves were suffering." The church is not a building. It is not an institution. It is not principally a meeting once a week. This has been recently demonstrated as we have continued to be the church even as in-person meetings were suspended for social distancing. The church is a body of people who are commissioned by God to be involved and engaged with one another.

I'll tell you what has stirred within me a newfound love for the church: I read the New Testament focused on the "one another" passages. Each time Scripture described something we Christians were meant to be providing "one another" as part of our life together, I took note.

Ephesians 4:12–16 has defined my perspective here. It says that as our leaders equip us, we will be ready to do works of service, "so that the body of Christ may be built up until we all reach unity in the faith and in the knowledge of the Son of God and become mature." Then, we are to speak the truth in love as we "grow to become in every respect the mature body of him who is the head, that is, Christ. From him the whole body, joined and held together by every supporting ligament, grows and builds itself up in love, as each part does its work."

The point here is that the goal of our faith is to be a healthy body, formed in the image of Jesus. This comes about as each part plays its role. I need you. You need me. We need all the other believers around us to be the body of Christ we are called to be. Our churches aren't supposed to be museums any more than they are supposed to be entertainment centers or social clubs. They are bodies of people using their gifts so everyone together takes on the image of Jesus.

Now, just let your mind run over some of the other things the Bible says we are meant to do to grow this corporate life. We are meant to serve each other. We are meant to love and challenge each other to become more like Christ. We're told to inspire each other to do good works. We are meant to use our unique individual gifts to provide for others and to help them conform to the example of Jesus. Those who teach should teach. Those who have gifts of generosity should give. And so it should go. We are also told to help each other out materially when the need arises. No one should go without. We are called to help each other fight off evil, remind each other of the truth, correct each other when it is needed, and treat each other as a family while we all grow up together in Jesus. All with the heart attitude to "be completely humble and gentle; be patient, bearing with one another in love."[24]

I could go on, but you get the point. The church is not a building. It is not a denomination. It is not a meeting. I know we say we are "going to church," and that is fine, as long as we know that what happens at ten o'clock on a Sunday morning is not "the church"; it's a meeting of the people who make up the church. Also, you aren't a devoted member of the body of Christ unless you are invested, unless you are giving and receiving all the magnificent gifts God has given us to build ourselves up into the mature image of Jesus Christ.

THE BLESSINGS OF FAITH AND COMMUNITY

Once we start to live this way, some pretty amazing dynamics kick in, dynamics that our whole society is waiting to see whether they realize it or not. When church "works"—in other words, when we stop *doing* church out of our own efforts and start *being* the church God commanded us and empowered us to be, we are building a loving, healing, restoring, inspiring, transforming environment like no other on earth. The results are so dramatic they can even be measured.

In a recent Harvard School of Public Health study published in the *American Journal of Epidemiology*, researchers discovered that individuals who went to church at least once a week when they were children or teens "were 18 percent more likely to report being happier in their twenties than those who never attended services." That's not all. People who went to church as children "were 33 percent less likely to use drugs in their twenties, were less likely to have sex at an earlier age, and less likely to have a sexually transmitted infection."[25]

There's more. "People who prayed and meditated daily either at church or on their own reported greater life satisfaction." They were better able to deal with and process their emotions and were far more forgiving. Researchers even discovered that those connected to church were less likely to smoke and far more likely to vote![26]

Read the final sentence of this research report, and remember that this is not coming from a religious publication: "Although decisions about religion are not shaped principally by health, for adolescents who already hold religious beliefs, encouraging service attendance and private practices may be meaningful avenues of development and support, possibly leading to better health and well-being."[27]

As our society continues to live out its dysfunctions and trauma, people will start looking for a haven. They will hunger for a place of rest, protection, healing, restoration, love, and belonging. The church is and has to be that place, but we can do it only if we understand at our core that church is a body of people loving each other and conforming together to the life and image of Jesus. #focusonthefuture

Now, if you are a churchgoer, you may already know this, and you can probably name many, many more benefits of going to church. But here is what is important about what I've just reported. These are the findings published by a non-Christian institution. In other words, the world outside the church recognizes that life in the church enhances the human experience in a variety of ways. This is important because as our society continues to live out its dysfunctions and trauma, people will start looking for a haven. They will hunger for a place of rest, protection, healing, restoration, love, and belonging. The church is and has to be that place, but we can do it only if we understand at our core that church is a body of people loving each other and conforming together to the life and image of Jesus.

A PEOPLE OF HOSPITALITY

This leads us to the next of our shifts and emphases that we will need to prepare for the future. We are going to have to master the biblical art of hospitality.

Now, be careful about how you think of this word. Our English word *hospitality* often refers to hotels, delicious meals, and people opening their homes and putting out a nice spread of food. We sometimes miss its intended meaning.

The New Testament word for *hospitality* or *hospitable* is a combination of two Greek words, *philos* meaning "loving, friendly" and *xénos* meaning "a stranger."[28] Biblical hospitality, then, is really about loving strangers. I certainly commend those who open their homes to fellow church members and care for them generously. Yet the hospitality we have to master is not primarily about people we already know or people we are necessarily comfortable with. It is about strangers, others, and people unlike us.

I've heard many church leaders say it this way: in the days to come, the Christian church is going to have to have a big front porch. Now, if you haven't lived in neighborhoods that had houses with porches, then you may not know what a porch can mean. A front porch on a house allows for people to drop by, have a seat, maybe have a refreshing drink or something to eat, and chat for a while. They don't have to go into the house. They can be friendly and get to know the family who lives in the house, all while staying in that middle ground between public space and private space called the porch.

I've seen the joy of a big old porch hundreds of times. It's where people get to know each other, discuss the business of the day or anything else attractive, and become friends in a relaxed, casual way. No appointments are necessary. No excuses have to be made to come and go. In short, the porch is a place where new folks and nonfamily are always welcome, a comfortable open space where once you arrive, you always belong if you want to.

That's why many of my church leader friends speak of churches having front porches or being community oriented. People want to belong before they believe.[29] Our goal has to be to give non-Christians a place to hang out with us without requiring them to join formally. Let them hang out in our culture for a while. Let them get the feel of who we are and what we are committed to. Let them have a laugh or two, build a few friendships, and sit at our dinner table for a while, so to speak—all without being pressured to "sign up." In other words, we build relationships and trust that the Holy Spirit is at work.

This is different from hospitality as we've known it and practiced it in our culture. In fact, in a powerful article in *Christianity Today* magazine, the author makes a helpful distinction between genuine biblical hospitality and entertainment:

> True hospitality is a cultural expression of other-oriented kingdom living. It transcends regional expectations of gourmet performance and focuses its energies on

the blessing of honest and sincere relationships. It isn't concerned with projecting an image of manicured lives devoid of stress, mess, and chaos. Instead, biblical hospitality flips the camera lens from a selfie to a wide-angle, pointed outward toward the lives of others, warmly inviting them into ours.[30]

The author goes on to develop four distinctions between biblical hospitality and mere entertainment. First, he says that entertainment seeks to impress, but biblical hospitality seeks to bless. Second, he contends that entertainment creates stress in pursuit of an ideal image, but genuine hospitality savors, offering rich, stressless experiences of God and friendship. Third, entertainment "babbles," filling the air with a lot of meaningless chatter. Yet hospitality, focused as it is on the guest, listens and tunes the heart to the needs and experiences of others. Finally, entertainment tends to exclude people and focus our attention on the least needy, but true, biblical hospitality honors people and isn't put off by the pain or inconveniences of others.[31]

> We need to learn this art of biblical hospitality in our churches because of what is coming. A traumatized, hurting, disoriented society is going to be forced by world events to reconsider God and His people. #focusonthefuture

We need to learn this art of biblical hospitality in our churches because of what is coming. A traumatized, hurting, disoriented society is going to be forced by world events to reconsider God and His people. But they are going to be skeptical. Many of them will be former church attenders who were hurt by their earlier experiences in the pews. Many will have read articles that raise questions about religious people. Still, they will come. They'll be looking for friendship. They'll be hoping not to feel pressured. They'll be eager for a welcome and a place of rest. As the Holy Spirit works in their lives, they'll find themselves gravitating to Jesus and the rich meaning of God's people doing life together. This is what the future looks like for us, and this is why we need to learn the craft of biblical hospitality on the big front porch of God's house.

THE PRESENCE OF GOD

Finally, and perhaps most importantly, to face what is coming, our churches are going to have to be places where God truly dwells. This may sound simplistic and like something so automatic that we don't have to be intentional about it. Trust me; it isn't.

When society begins to flood into our churches, we want them to encounter the living God. We want them to hear a Spirit-empowered gospel and live among a people who live in the power of God. They are going to come hungry and hurting and desperate. We will have to have resources beyond our own. We will have to be skilled not only in introducing people to Jesus but also in healing trauma, restoring families, building strong men and women, and making trustworthy disciples able to change a sick and dying culture.

This means we will have to be a Jesus-centered people. I have always loved a quote from the great C.S. Lewis. He once wrote, "The perfect church service would be one we were almost unaware of; our attention would have been on God."[32] In much the same sense, this is what our churches need to become. We want God so enthroned in the midst of us that outsiders fall on their knees and say, "Surely God is among you." In other words, we don't want our churches to be mere human experiences. We want them to be divine experiences. We want the aching souls of people to be filled with what they find among us. We want people to meet Jesus, not just at the end of a sermon, but in the life we share in God.

> We don't want our churches to be mere human experiences. We want them to be divine experiences. We want the aching souls of people to be filled with what they find among us. We want people to meet Jesus, not just at the end of a sermon, but in the life we share in God. #focusonthefuture

This is what it will mean for us to be a bride who has made herself ready. It will mean repentance and rebuilding. It will mean prayer and fasting. It will involve working hard to be a biblical people and then working hard again to be a generous, stranger-loving people. Yet if we do these things, we will be the people we are called to be for our generation, a people genuinely fulfilling their purpose for such a time as this. God be with you. God be with us. The future is now.

NOTES

INTRODUCTION

1. Lamentations 1:9.
2. "The Roman Empire in the First Century," PBS, accessed June 23, 2020, https://calvarychapel.com/posts/the-early-church-how-christianity-revolutionized-sexual-morality.
3. Paul Carter, "How Did Christianity Take Over the Ancient World? (And Could It Happen Again?)," The Gospel Coalition Canada, November 11, 2018, https://ca.thegospelcoalition.org/columns/ad-fontes/how-did-christianity-take-over-the-ancient-world-and-could-it-happen-again/.
4. Jasmine Alnutt, "The Early Church: How Christianity Revolutionized the Depravity of Roman Culture," Calvary Chapel, March 28, 2017, https://calvarychapel.com/posts/the-early-church-how-christianity-revolutionized-sexual-morality.
5. See 1 Corinthians 6:1–2.
6. "History of Tribunals," Archdiocese of Cincinnati, accessed June 23, 2020, http://www.catholiccincinnati.org/ministries-offices/tribunal/history-of-tribunal/.
7. Jean Carlos Zukowski, "The Role and Status of the Catholic Church in the Church-State Relationship Within the Roman Empire From A.D. 306 to 814," Andrews University, 2009, https://digitalcommons.andrews.edu/cgi/viewcontent.cgi?article=1173&context=dissertations.

CHAPTER 1

1. John Adams, *Letters of John Adams, Addressed to His Wife*, vol. 1, ed. Charles F. Adams, (Boston: Charles C. Little, and James Brown, 1841), 218.

2. Dallas Willard, *The Spirit of the Disciplines: Understanding How God Changes Lives* (San Francisco: HarperSanFrancisco, 1988), viii.

3. George Gallup Jr. and Timothy K. Jones, *The Next American Spirituality: Finding God in the Twenty-First Century* (Colorado Springs: Victor, 2000), 29.

4. "Dr. Dobson's December Newsletter," Dr. James Dobson's Family Talk, accessed June 23, 2020, http://www.drjamesdobson.org/news/commentaries/archives/2017-newsletters/december-newsletter-2017.

5. Esther 4:14.

6. Micah 6:8.

7. Rita Dunaway, *Restoring America's Soul* (Herndon, VA: Mascot Books, 2019), chap. 5, Kindle.

CHAPTER 2

1. Eric J. Lyman, "Pope, Obama Visit Should Be Cordial Despite Differences," *USA Today*, March 26, 2014, https://web.archive.org/web/20171118235025/https://www.usatoday.com/story/news/world/2014/03/26/obama-pope-vatican/6874965/.

2. Children's Bureau, "Child Maltreatment 2018," January 15, 2020, ii, x, https://www.acf.hhs.gov/sites/default/files/cb/cm2018.pdf.

3. "Victims of Sexual Violence: Statistics," *RAINN*, accessed June 3, 2020, https://www.rainn.org/statistics/victims-sexual-violence.

4. "The National Intimate Partner and Sexual Violence Survey: 2010 Summary Report," Centers for Disease Control and Prevention, National Center for Injury Prevention and Control, November 2011, https://www.cdc.gov/violenceprevention/pdf/nisvs_report2010-a.pdf.

5. "Infertility FAQs," Centers for Disease Control and Prevention, last reviewed January 16, 2019, https://www.cdc.gov/reproductivehealth/infertility/index.htm.

6. "Ten Years of Mass Shootings in the United States: An Everytown for Gun Safety Support Fund Analysis," Everytown, November 21, 2019, https://everytownresearch.org/massshootingsreports/mass-shootings-in-america-2009-2019/.

7. Jamie Ducharme, "US Suicide Rates Are the Highest They've Been Since World War II," *Time*, June 20, 2019, https://time.com/5609124/us-suicide-rate-increase/.

8. Ducharme, "US Suicide Rates Are the Highest They've Been Since World War II."

9. Ducharme, "US Suicide Rates Are the Highest They've Been Since World War II."

10. "Booze Buying Surges; Senators Push Airlines for Cash Refunds," AP News, March 31, 2020, https://apnews.com/c407ecb931c6c528b4cceb0ecc216f0c.

11. Ashley Kirzinger et al., "KFF Health Tracking Poll—Early April 2020: The Impact of Coronavirus on Life in America," Kaiser Family Foundation, April 2, 2020, https://www.kff.org/health-reform/report/kff-health-tracking-poll-early-april-2020/.

12. Kouichi Yoshimasu et al., "Suicidal Risk Factors and Completed Suicide: Meta-analyses Based on Psychological Autopsy Studies," *Environmental Health and Preventive Medicine* 13, no. 5 (2008): 243–56, https://www.ncbi.nlm.nih.gov/pmc/articles/PMC2698248/.

13. Michael Gerson, "Suicides Are at an All Time High. We Need Hope More Than Ever," *Washington Post*, June 20, 2019, https://www.washingtonpost.com/opinions/suicides-are-at-an-all-time-high-we-need-hope-more-than-ever/2019/06/20/b591702e-9396-11e9-b58a-a6a9afaa0e3e_story.html.

14. Scott Higham, Sari Horwitz, and Steven Rich, "76 Billion Opioid Pills: Newly Released Federal Data Unmasks the Epidemic," *Washington Post*, July 16, 2019, https://www.washingtonpost.com/

investigations/76-billion-opioid-pills-newly-released-federal-data-unmasks-the-epidemic/2019/07/16/5f29fd62-a73e-11e9-86dd-d7f0e60391e9_story.html.

15. "Pain Management and the Opioid Epidemic: Balancing Societal and Individual Benefits and Risks of Prescription Opioid Use," NCBI, accessed June 23, 2020, https://www.ncbi.nlm.nih.gov/books/NBK458661/.

16. John Paul II, "Homily of John Paul II" (sermon, Perth, Australia, November 30, 1986), https://w2.vatican.va/content/john-paul-ii/en/homilies/1986/documents/hf_jp-ii_hom_19861130_perth-australia.html.

17. Dunaway, *Restoring America's Soul*, chap. 1.

18. Abraham Lincoln, "The National Fast; Proclamation by the President of the United States," *New York Times*, April 30, 1863, https://www.nytimes.com/1863/04/30/archives/the-national-fast-proclamation-by-the-president-of-the-united.html.

CHAPTER 3

1. Dale Buss, *Family Man: The Biography of James Dobson* (Carol Stream, IL: Tyndale, 2005), 18.

2. Buss, *Family Man*, 28–30.

3. Irving B. Weiner and W. Edward Craighead, eds., *The Corsini Encyclopedia of Psychology*, 4th ed., vol. 4 (Hoboken, NJ: John Wiley & Sons, 2010), 1452, https://books.google.com/books?id=pUSG1BONmekC.

4. Paul C. Vitz, *Psychology as Religion: The Cult of Self-Worship*, 2nd ed. (Grand Rapids: William B. Eerdmans, 1994), 3.

5. David D. Kirkpatrick, "Evangelical Leader Threatens to Use His Political Muscle Against Some Democrats," *New York Times*, January 1, 2005, https://www.nytimes.com/2005/01/01/politics/evangelical-leader-threatens-to-use-his-political-muscle-against.html.

6. Dan Valentine, "What Is a School?," *Salt Lake Tribune,* September 5, 1967, https://www.newspapers.com/ clip/1064138/the-salt-lake-tribune/.

7. "What Most Influences the Self-Identity of Americans?," Barna Group, March 19, 2015, https://www.barna.com/ research/what-most-influences-the-self-identity-of-americans/.

8. Emily Kent Smith, "Youngsters as Young as 11 'Addicted' to Online Porn as 2,000 Children Seek Counselling Having Viewed Sickening Material While Surfing the Web," *Daily Mail,* March 15, 2018, https://www. dailymail.co.uk/news/article-5507751/NSPCC-offers-counselling-children-young-11-addicted-porn.html.

9. Marla E. Eisenberg et al., "Correlations Between Family Meals and Psychological Well-Being Among Adolescents," *Archives of Pediatrics and Adolescent Medicine* 158, no. 8 (August 2004): 792–96, https:// jamanetwork.com/journals/jamapediatrics/ fullarticle/485781.

10. "The Importance of Family Dinners V," National Center on Addiction and Substance Abuse at Columbia University (CASA), September 2009, PDF download, 2, https://www.centeronaddiction.org/addiction-research/ reports/importance-of-family-dinners-2009.

11. Matthew W. Gillman et al., "Family Dinner and Diet Quality Among Older Children and Adolescents," *Archives of Family Medicine* 9, no. 3 (2000): 235–40, https://pubmed.ncbi.nlm.nih.gov/10728109/.

12. Amber J. Hammons and Barbara H. Fiese, "Is Frequency of Shared Family Meals Related to the Nutritional Health of Children and Adolescents?," *Pediatrics* 127, no. 6 (June 2011): e1565–74, https://www.ncbi.nlm.nih.gov/ pmc/articles/PMC3387875/.

13. Patrick A. Coleman, "6 Reasons Family Dinners Are Important for Your Child," *Fatherly,* February 8, 2017,

https://www.fatherly.com/health-science/6-reasons-eating-family-dinner/.

14. Trent Hamm, "Don't Eat Out as Often (188/365)," The Simple Dollar, updated April 13. 2020, https://www.thesimpledollar.com/save-money/dont-eat-out-as-often/.

15. Tim Clinton, "From the Heart: Hold Hands While You Sleep," *Christian Counseling Today*.

16. Genesis 2:23.

17. Michael Layne, "Unending Love: Elderly Couple Die on Same Day While Holding Hands," GodTV, April 24, 2019, https://godtv.com/unending-love-couple-die-on-same-day-while-holding-hands/.

18. Luke 17:1, KJV.

19. Hebrews 12:15, KJV.

20. "Married Couples & Parents See Fewer Barriers to Forgiving Others," Barna Group, June 11, 2019, https://www.barna.com/research/married-parents-forgiving-others/.

21. "Married Couples & Parents See Fewer Barriers to Forgiving Others," Barna Group.

22. "Married Couples & Parents See Fewer Barriers to Forgiving Others," Barna Group.

23. "Married Couples & Parents See Fewer Barriers to Forgiving Others," Barna Group.

24. "Why People Fight Online," Barna Group, May 18, 2017, https://www.barna.com/research/people-fight-online/.

25. "Why People Fight Online," Barna Group.

26. Dave Ramsey, "Yea, Too many people with no class and digital courage," Twitter, August 26, 2018, https://twitter.com/DaveRamsey/status/1033697722925285376.

27. "Why People Fight Online," Barna Group.

28. Michael Hyatt, "The Secret to Ben Carson's Success," Michael Hyatt & Co., updated September 18, 2015, https://michaelhyatt.com/ben-carson-reading/.

29. "What Makes for a Spiritually Vibrant Household?," Barna Group, March 5, 2019, https://www.barna.com/research/spiritually-vibrant-household/.

30. "What Makes for a Spiritually Vibrant Household?," Barna Group.

31. "What Makes for a Spiritually Vibrant Household?," Barna Group.

32. "What Makes for a Spiritually Vibrant Household?," Barna Group.

33. W. Bradford Wilcox and Nicholas H. Wolfinger, "Better Together: Religious Attendance, Gender, and Relationship Quality," Institute for Family Studies, February 11, 2016, https://ifstudies.org/blog/better-together-religious-attendance-gender-and-relationship-quality.

34. Wilcox and Wolfinger, "Better Together."

CHAPTER 4

1. Genesis 45:3, 13.

2. 2 Timothy 4:9, 13.

3. Malachi 4:6.

4. Linda Bird Francke, "The Sons of Divorce," *New York Times Magazine*, May 22, 1983, https://www.nytimes.com/1983/05/22/magazine/the-sons-of-divorce.html.

5. 1 Kings 2:2, KJV.

6. Olivia Campbell, "The Men Taking Classes to Unlearn Toxic Masculinity," The Cut, October 23, 2017, https://www.thecut.com/2017/10/the-men-taking-classes-to-unlearn-toxic-masculinity.html.

7. Mark Hensch, "Clinton: 'Deep-Seated' Beliefs Block Abortion Access," *The Hill*, April 24, 2015, http://thehill.com/blogs/ballot-box/239974-clinton-deep-seated-beliefs-block-abortion-access.

8. Stephanie Pappas, "APA Issues First-Ever Guidelines for Practice with Men and Boys," *American Psychological*

Association 50, no. 1 (2019), https://www.apa.org/ monitor/2019/01/ce-corner.

9. Pappas, "APA Issues First-Ever Guidelines for Practice with Men and Boys."

10. Rod Dreher, "Manhood as Mental Disorder," *The American Conservative*, January 7, 2019, https://www. theamericanconservative.com/dreher/manhood-as-mental-disorder/.

11. Geoffrey Miller, Twitter, January 6, 2019, https://twitter. com/primalpoly/status/1081993778481655808.

12. American Psychological Association, *APA Guidelines for Psychological Practice with Boys and Men*, August 2018, https://www.apa.org/about/policy/boys-men-practice-guidelines.pdf.

13. Jordan Peterson, "Jordan Peterson: It's Ideology vs. Science in Psychology's War on Boys and Men," *National Post*, February 1, 2019, https://nationalpost. com/opinion/jordan-peterson-its-ideology-vs-science-in-psychologys-war-on-boys-and-men.

14. Stephanie Kramer, "U.S. Has World's Highest Rate of Children Living in Single-Parent Households," Pew Research Center, December 12, 2019, https://www. pewresearch.org/fact-tank/2019/12/12/u-s-children-more-likely-than-children-in-other-countries-to-live-with-just-one-parent/.

15. Brittany Wallman et al., "A Lost and Lonely Killer," *Sun Sentinel*, February 24, 2018, https://www.sun-sentinel. com/local/broward/parkland/florida-school-shooting/ fl-florida-school-shooting-nikolas-cruz-life-20180220-story.html.

16. Frances Robles and Nikita Stewart, "Dylann Roof's Past Reveals Trouble at Home and School," *New York Times*, July 16, 2015, https://www.nytimes.com/2015/07/17/us/ charleston-shooting-dylann-roof-troubled-past.html.

17. Marc Santora, "Sandy Hook Gunman's Father Says He Wishes His Son Had Never Been Born," *New York Times*,

March 10, 2014, https://www.nytimes.com/2014/03/11/nyregion/adam-lanzas-father-in-first-public-comments-says-you-cant-get-any-more-evil.html.

18. Jay Ambrose, "Fatherless Homes a Factor in Mass Shootings," *Sun Sentinel*, March 1, 2018, https://www.sun-sentinel.com/opinion/fl-op-mass-shootings-fatherless-homes-20180227-story.html.

19. "Research and Statistics," Rochester Area Fatherhood Network, accessed June 6, 2020, http://www.rochesterareafatherhoodnetwork.org/statistics#.

20. "Research and Statistics," Rochester Area Fatherhood Network.

21. "Research and Statistics," Rochester Area Fatherhood Network.

22. Tim Clinton, "Imaginary Lovers," *Christian Counseling Today* 22, no. 1 (2014).

23. Chiara Sabina, Janis Wolak, and David Finkelhor, "The Nature and Dynamics of Internet Pornography Exposure for Youth," *CyberPsychology and Behavior* 11, no. 6 (2008): 691-93, http://www.unh.edu/ccrc/pdf/CV169.pdf.

24. "Age of First Exposure to Pornography Shapes Men's Attitudes Toward Women," American Psychological Association, August 3, 2017, http://apa.org/news/press/releases/2017/08/pornography-exposure.aspx.

25. "Consider This: Digging Deeper," Novus Project, accessed June 6, 2020, http://thenovusproject.org/resource-hub/parents.

26. "Children and Pornography," Digital Kids Initiative, Center for Parent/Youth Understanding, 2020, https://digitalkidsinitiative.com/wp-content/uploads/2020/04/Children_and_Pornography_Factsheet-Updated-2020.pdf.

27. Josh McDowell, "Executive Summary," *The Porn Epidemic: Facts, Stats, and Solutions*, September 25, 2018, 2, https://www.josh.org/wp-content/uploads/Porn-Epidemic-Executive-Summary-9.25.2018.pdf.

28. Tim Clinton, "From the Heart: Boys to Men," *Christian Counseling Today* 23, no. 1 (2015).
29. "The Lost Boys of Sudan," International Rescue Committee, October 3, 2014, https://www.rescue.org/article/lost-boys-sudan.
30. Clinton, "From the Heart: Boys to Men."
31. "New Report Finds Teens Feel Addicted to Their Phones, Causing Tension at Home," Common Sense Media, May 3, 2016, https://www.commonsensemedia.org/about-us/news/press-releases/new-report-finds-teens-feel-addicted-to-their-phones-causing-tension-at.
32. Victor C. Strasburger, "Children, Adolescents, and the Media," *Current Problems in Pediatric and Adolescent Health Care* 34, no. 2 (2004): 64, https://www.researchgate.net/publication/6935595_Children_adolescents_and_the_media.
33. Janis Wolak, Kimberly Mitchell, and David Finkelhor, "Unwanted and Wanted Exposure to Online Pornography in a National Sample of Youth Internet Users," *Pediatrics* 119, no. 2 (February 2007): 247–57, http://www.unh.edu/ccrc/pdf/CV153.pdf.
34. Kaiser Family Foundation et al., *National Survey of Adolescents and Young Adults: Sexual Health Knowledge, Attitudes, and Experiences* (Menlo Park, CA: Henry J. Kaiser Family Foundation, 2003), 37, https://www.kff.org/wp-content/uploads/2013/01/national-survey-of-adolescents-and-young-adults.pdf.
35. Kevin Leapley, "Facts About Pornography," Front Range Counseling Center, February 23, 2014, https://www.frontrangecounselingcenter.com/facts-pornography/.
36. Clinton, "From the Heart: Boys to Men."
37. 1 Corinthians 16:13, ESV.
38. Gretchen Livingston and Kim Parker, "8 Facts About American Dads," Pew Research Center, June 12, 2019, https://www.pewresearch.org/fact-tank/2019/06/12/fathers-day-facts/.

39. Gallup Poll, "Father Figures," National Center for Fathering, 1996, quoted in "The Effects of FatherFULLness," Fathers.com, accessed June 11, 2020, http://fathers.com/statistics-and-research/the-effects-of-fatherfullness/.

40. Ladan Nikravan Hayes, "Working Dads Feel They Can Have It All," June 13, 2018, https://resources.careerbuilder.com/news-research/working-dads-can-have-it-all.

41. Ephesians 6:4, KJV.

42. "Research and Statistics," Rochester Area Fatherhood Network.

43. James R. Dudley and Glenn Stone, *Fathering at Risk: Helping Nonresidential Fathers* (New York: Springer Publishing, 2001), 70, https://books.google.com/books?id=b5HSCgAAQBAJ&pg.

44. Meg Meeker, *Strong Fathers, Strong Daughters: 10 Secrets Every Father Should Know* (New York: Ballantine Books, 2007), 24, https://books.google.com/books?id=U06fudQ8CrAC&q.

45. Bob Horner, Ron Ralston, and David Sunde, *The Promise Keeper at Work* (Nashville: Word Publishing, 1999), 111.

46. European Population Committee, "The Demographic Characteristics of National Minorities in Certain European States: The Demographic Characteristics of Linguistic and Religious Groups in Switzerland," CM(99)138 Addendum 5, table 9, October 27, 1999, https://rm.coe.int/16804fb7b1.

47. James Dobson, "Murder and Mayhem. What's Going on Out There?," Family Talk newsletter, September 2019, https://www.drjamesdobson.org/news/commentaries/archives/2019-newsletters/september-newsletter-2019.

CHAPTER 5

1. Genesis 2:18.

2. Terry McCarthy, "Getting Inside Your Head," *Time*, October 16, 2005, http://labs.vtc.vt.edu/hnl/cache/time_gettingInsideHead.htm.

3. McCarthy, "Getting Inside Your Head."

4. John J. Ratey, *A User's Guide to the Brain: Perception, Attention, and the Four Theaters of the Brain* (New York: Vintage Books, 2002), 3, https://www.google.com/books/edition/_/DgiPDQAAQBAJ?hl=en&gbpv=0.

5. Lisa Pauwels, Sima Chalavi, and Stephan P. Swinnen, "Aging and Brain Plasticity," *Aging* 10, no. 8 (2018): 1789–90, https://www.ncbi.nlm.nih.gov/pmc/articles/PMC6128435/.

6. Riitta Hari et al., "Centrality of Social Interaction in Human Brain Function," *Neuron* 88, no. 1 (October 7, 2015): 181–93, https://www.sciencedirect.com/science/article/pii/S0896627315007795.

7. Sylvia A. Morelli, Jared B. Torre, and Naomi I. Eisenberger, "The Neural Bases of Feeling Understood and Not Understood," *Social Cognitive and Affective Neuroscience* 9, no. 12 (December 2014): 1890–96 https://academic.oup.com/scan/article/9/12/1890/1615491; "Anti-anxiety Medications (Benzodiazepines)," Centre for Addiction and Mental Health, 2012, https://www.camh.ca/en/health-info/mental-illness-and-addiction-index/anti-anxiety-medications-benzodiazepines.

8. "About Mindsight," Dr. Dan Siegel, accessed June 8, 2020, https://www.drdansiegel.com/about/mindsight/.

9. Matthew 7:12.

10. Gregor Domes et al., "Autistic Traits and Empathy in Chronic vs. Episodic Depression," *Journal of Affective Disorders* 195 (May 2016): 144–47, https://www.sciencedirect.com/science/article/abs/pii/S0165032715310314.

11. Brendan D. Hare and Ronald S Duman, "Prefrontal Cortex Circuits in Depression and Anxiety: Contribution of Discrete Neuronal Populations and

Target Regions," *Molecular Psychiatry*, February 21, 2020, https://pubmed.ncbi.nlm.nih.gov/32086434/; McGill University, "Promising Advance in Depression Research: Identification of Key Protein May Lead to More Effective Anti-Depressants," ScienceDaily, April 8, 2020, https://www.sciencedaily.com/releases/2020/04/200408113245.htm.

12. Elizabeth Williams, "Research Reveals: The More You Hug Your Kids, The Smarter They Become," *Curious Mind Magazine*, accessed June 9, 2020, https://curiousmindmagazine.com/research-reveals-hug-kids-smarter-become/.

13. Williams, "Research Reveals."

14. Cell Press, "A Prescription for Touch: Early Experiences Shape Preterm Babies' Brains," ScienceDaily, March 16, 2017, https://www.sciencedaily.com/releases/2017/03/170316120502.htm.

15. Williams, "Research Reveals."

16. Child Welfare Information Gateway, *Understanding the Effects of Maltreatment on Brain Development* (Washington, DC: U.S. Department of Health and Human Services, Children's Bureau, 2015), https://www.childwelfare.gov/pubPDFs/brain_development.pdf.

17. Daniel J. Siegel, *The Mindful Brain: Reflection and Attunement in the Cultivation of Well-Being* (New York: W. W. Norton, 2007), 5, https://www.amazon.com/Mindful-Brain-Reflection-Attunement-Cultivation/dp/039370470X.

18. Curt Thompson, *The Soul of Shame: Retelling the Stories We Believe About Ourselves* (Downers Grove: InterVarsity Press, 2015), 40, https://www.google.com/books/edition/The_Soul_of_Shame/zDyfCgAAQBAJ.

19. Werner Mischke, "Toxic Shame Has Its Own Neurobiology. The Gospel Offers a Cure," *Culture Learner* (blog), August 8, 2018, https://wernermischke.org/2018/08/08/

toxic-shame-has-its-own-neurobiology-the-gospel-offers-a-cure/.

20. Mischke, "Toxic Shame Has Its Own Neurobiology. The Gospel Offers a Cure."

21. Mischke, "Toxic Shame Has Its Own Neurobiology. The Gospel Offers a Cure."

22. Thompson, *The Soul of Shame*, 173–74.

23. Louis Cozolino, "Nine Things Educators Need to Know About the Brain," *Greater Good Magazine*, March 19, 2013, https://greatergood.berkeley.edu/article/item/nine_things_educators_need_to_know_about_the_brain.

24. Daniel J. Siegel, "How Social Media Is Rewiring Our Brains," Science Insider, January 15, 2015, video, 0:22–1:17, https://www.youtube.com/watch?v=CkMh6xdJNeM.

25. Siegel, "How Social Media Is Rewiring Our Brains," 1:38–2:15.

26. Siegel, "How Social Media Is Rewiring Our Brains," 2:15–2:25.

27. Siegel, "How Social Media Is Rewiring Our Brains," 2:25–2:50.

28. Siegel, "How Social Media Is Rewiring Our Brains," 2:51–3:21.

29. Siegel, "How Social Media Is Rewiring Our Brains," 3:22–4:00.

30. Betsy Mikel, "Science Says: This Could Be Why Millennials Are Having Less Sex," *Inc.*, March 14, 2017, https://www.inc.com/betsy-mikel/science-says-this-could-be-why-millennials-are-having-less-sex.html.

31. Michael Dimock, "Where Millennials End and Generation Z Begins," Pew Research Center, January 17, 2019, https://www.pewresearch.org/fact-tank/2019/01/17/where-millennials-end-and-generation-z-begins/.

32. Brian Resnick, "22 Percent of Millennials Say They Have 'No Friends,'" *Vox*, August 1, 2019, https://www.vox.com/science-and-health/2019/8/1/20750047/millennials-poll-loneliness.

33. Resnick, "22 Percent of Millennials Say They Have 'No Friends.'"

34. "U.S. Adults Have Few Friends—and They're Mostly Alike," Barna, October 23, 2018, https://www.barna.com/research/friends-loneliness/.

35. "US Adults Have Few Friends—and They're Mostly Alike," Barna.

36. "US Adults Have Few Friends—and They're Mostly Alike," Barna.

37. "US Adults Have Few Friends—and They're Mostly Alike," Barna.

38. "US Adults Have Few Friends—and They're Mostly Alike," Barna.

39. Tim Clinton, "The Road to Nowhere: All The Day," *Christian Counseling Today* 23, no. 2.

40. Rob Price, "Apple CEO Tim Cook: I Don't Want My Nephew on Social Media," *Business Insider*, January 19, 2018, https://www.businessinsider.com/apple-ceo-tim-cook-doesnt-let-nephew-use-social-media-2018-1.

41. "New Report Finds Teens Feel Addicted to Their Phones, Causing Tension at Home," Common Sense Media.

42. Mary Madden and Lee Rainie, "Major Findings," Pew Research Center, June 18, 2010, http://www.pewinternet.org/2010/06/18/major-findings/.

43. Alice G. Walton, "Phone Addiction Is Real—And So Are Its Mental Health Risks," *Forbes*, December 11, 2017, https://www.forbes.com/sites/alicegwalton/2017/12/11/phone-addiction-is-real-and-so-are-its-mental-health-risks/#5a00ee0f13df.

44. Clinton, "The Road to Nowhere: All The Day."

45. "Matthew 28:20," Bible Hub, accessed June 23, 2020, https://biblehub.com/commentaries/matthew/28-20.htm.

CHAPTER 6

1. 2 Kings 20:13, NKJV.

2. 2 Kings 20:15, NKJV.
3. 2 Kings 20:16–18, NKJV.
4. 2 Kings 20:19.
5. Stephanie Coontz, *The Way We Never Were: American Families and the Nostalgia Trap* (New York: BasicBooks, 1992), 3, https://books.google.com/books?id=cCgbAAAAYAAJ.
6. "Abortion," Gallup, accessed June 10, 2020, https://news.gallup.com/poll/1576/abortion.aspx.
7. Don E. Fehrenbacher and Virginia Fehrenbacher, eds., *Recollected Words of Abraham Lincoln* (Stanford: Stanford University Press, 1996), 240.
8. "Abraham Lincoln Historical Digitization Project," Northern Illinois University Digital Library, accessed August 4, 2021, https://digital.lib.niu.edu/islandora/object/niu-lincoln%3A35801, chapter 8.
9. Sean McDowell, "9 Important Insights About Generation Z," SeanMcDowell.org, November 29, 2016, https://seanmcdowell.org/blog/9-important-insights-about-generation-z.
10. S. McDowell, "9 Important Insights About Generation Z."
11. Bernard Schroeder, "A Majority of Gen Z Aspires to Be Entrepreneurs and Perhaps Delay or Skip College. Why That Might Be a Good Idea," *Forbes*, February 18, 2020, https://www.forbes.com/sites/bernhardschroeder/2020/02/18/a-majority-of-gen-z-aspires-to-be-entrepreneurs-and-perhaps-delay-or-skip-college-why-that-might-be-a-good-idea/.
12. S. McDowell, "9 Important Insights About Generation Z."
13. Anne Fisher, "Forget Millennials. Are You Ready to Hire Generation Z?" *Fortune*, August 14, 2016, https://fortune.com/2016/08/14/generation-z-employers/.
14. Richard Fry and Kim Parker, "Early Benchmarks Show 'Post-Millennials' on Track to Be Most Diverse,

Best-Educated Generation Yet," Pew Research Center, November 15, 2018, https://www.pewsocialtrends. org/2018/11/15/early-benchmarks-show-post-millennials-on-track-to-be-most-diverse-best-educated-generation-yet/.

15. Alex Williams, "Move Over, Millennials, Here Comes Generation Z," *New York Times*, September 18, 2015, https://www.nytimes.com/2015/09/20/fashion/move-over-millennials-here-comes-generation-z.html.

16. S. McDowell, "9 Important Insights About Generation Z."

17. Kevin Eagan et al., *The American Freshman: Fifty-Year Trends, 1966–2015* (Los Angeles: Higher Education Research Institute, UCLA, 2016), 7, https://www.heri. ucla.edu/monographs/50YearTrendsMonograph2016.pdf.

18. S. McDowell, "9 Important Insights About Generation Z."

19. S. McDowell, "9 Important Insights About Generation Z."

20. S. McDowell, "9 Important Insights About Generation Z."

21. S. McDowell, "9 Important Insights About Generation Z."

22. "Mental Health in America—Youth Data: Youth Ranking 2020," Mental Health America, accessed June 12, 2020, https://www.mhanational.org/issues/mental-health-america-youth-data#two.

23. Susanna Schrobsdorff, "Teen Depression and Anxiety: Why the Kids Are Not All Right," *Time*, October 27, 2016, https://time.com/4547322/american-teens-anxious-depressed-overwhelmed/.

24. S. McDowell, "9 Important Insights About Generation Z."

25. Schrobsdorff, "Teen Depression and Anxiety."

26. Erin Anderssen, "Through the Eyes of Generation Z," *The Globe and Mail*, June 24, 2016, https://www.

theglobeandmail.com/news/national/through-the-eyes-of-generation-z/article30571914/.

27. "Mental Health Facts: Children and Teens," National Alliance on Mental Illness, 2016, https://www.nami.org/nami/media/nami-media/infographics/children-mh-facts-nami.pdf.

28. Stephen Colbert, "If Politicians Won't Take Action, These High Schoolers Will," *The Late Show with Stephen Colbert*, NBC, February 20, 2018, video, 3:12, https://www.youtube.com/watch?v=Oa0tSw2iV5o.

29. Ashley Stahl, "Why Democrats Should Be Losing Sleep Over Generation Z," *Forbes*, August 11, 2017, https://www.forbes.com/sites/ashleystahl/2017/08/11/why-democrats-should-be-losing-sleep-over-generation-z/.

30. Stahl, "Why Democrats Should Be Losing Sleep Over Generation Z."

31. Denise Villa and Jason Dorsey, "The State of Gen Z 2017," The Center for Generational Kinetics, April 2017, https://genhq.com/gen-z-2017-research-white-paper/.

32. Villa and Dorsey, "The State of Gen Z 2017."

33. "New National Study: The State of Gen Z 2017," The Center for Generational Kinetics, accessed June 12, 2020, https://genhq.com/new-natiBarnaonal-study-state-gen-z-2017/.

34. Eric Spitznagel, "Generation Z Is Bigger Than Millennials—And They're Out to Change the World," *New York Post*, January 25, 2020, https://nypost.com/2020/01/25/generation-z-is-bigger-than-millennials-and-theyre-out-to-change-the-world/.

35. Erin Duffin, "Resident Population in the United States in 2017, by Generation," *Statista*, August 9, 2019, https://www.statista.com/statistics/797321/us-population-by-generation/.

36. "The Powerful Influence of Moms in Christians' Households," Barna Group, May 7, 2019, https://www.barna.com/research/moms-christians-households/.

37. "The Powerful Influence of Moms in Christians' Households," Barna Group.

38. "The Powerful Influence of Moms in Christians' Households," Barna Group.

39. "The Powerful Influence of Moms in Christians' Households," Barna Group.

40. Studylight.org, s.v. "'êm," accessed June 14, 2020, https://www.studylight.org/lexicons/hebrew/517.html.

41. Proverbs 1:8.

42. See John 19:26–27.

43. Drew G. Faust, "The Civil War Soldier and the Art of Dying," *Journal of Southern History* 67, no.1 (February 2001): 26n35, https://dash.harvard.edu/handle/1/2634148.

44. James Dobson, *Bringing Up Boys* (Carol Stream, IL: Tyndale Momentum, 2005), 102, 245–46, https://books.google.com/books?id=hZVUBAAAQBAJ.

45. Charles R. Swindoll, *Growing Strong in the Seasons of Life* (Grand Rapids: Zondervan, 1994), 71.

46. Proverbs 22:6, ESV.

47. Bible Hub, "Proverbs 22:6," accessed June 14, 2020, https://biblehub.com/commentaries/proverbs/22-6.htm.

48. Tim Kimmel, *Grace-Based Parenting: Set Your Family Free* (Nashville: Thomas Nelson, 2004), 111–12, https://books.google.com/books?id=Qscqm5jecXQC.

49. Proverbs 22:15, KJV.

50. Grace Ketterman, "Godly Parenting," *The Care and Counsel Bible* (Nashville: Thomas Nelson, 2001), 830–31.

51. Esther 4:14.

CHAPTER 7

1. Exodus 20:5.

2. Exodus 20:6.

3. Winston Churchill, "Their Finest Hour," June 18, 1940, https://winstonchurchill.org/resources/speeches/1940-the-finest-hour/their-finest-hour/.

4. Open Doors, *World Watch List 2020* (Santa Ana, CA: Open Doors, 2020), 3–5, https://www.opendoorsusa.org/wp-content/uploads/2020/01/2020_World_Watch_List.pdf.

5. Jonathan Merritt, "'Double Persecution': The Untold Plight of Christian Women Worldwide," *Religion News Service*, January 10, 2018, https://religionnews.com/2018/01/10/double-persecution-the-untold-plight-of-christian-women-worldwide/.

6. Masterpiece Cakeshop, Ltd. v. Colorado Civil Rights Commission, 584 U.S. 2 (2018).

7. Alana LaFlore, "Complaint Made About Prayer Before Bradley Central Football Game," News Channel 9, January 21, 2018, https://newschannel9.com/news/local/complaint-made-about-prayer-before-bradley-central-football-game.

8. "Most Christians View Their Faith as a Force for Good," Barna Report, March 16, 2016, https://www.barna.com/research/most-christians-view-their-faith-as-a-force-for-good/.

9. Lauren Camera, "U.S. Students Show No Improvement in Math, Reading, Science on International Exam," *U.S. News and World Report*, December 3, 2019, https://www.usnews.com/news/education-news/articles/2019-12-03/us-students-show-no-improvement-in-math-reading-science-on-international-exam.

10. "Public Schools: Christians Are Part of the Solution," Barna Report, August 26, 2014, https://www.barna.com/research/public-schools-christians-are-part-of-the-solution/.

11. "Public Schools," Barna Report.

12. "Public Schools," Barna Report.

13. Studylight.org, s.v. *"euangélion,"* accessed June 14, 2020, https://www.studylight.org/lexicons/greek/2098.html.

14. Deuteronomy 31:6.

15. Philippians 1:28.

16. Acts 4:13.

17. Bob Smietana, "Americans Are Fond of the Bible, Don't Actually Read It," LifeWay Research, April 25, 2017, https://lifewayresearch.com/2017/04/25/lifeway-research-americans-are-fond-of-the-bible-dont-actually-read-it/.
18. Romans 12:2.
19. John 6:63.

CHAPTER 8

1. Alexis de Tocqueville, *Democracy in America*, vol. 1 (New York, 1899: Project Gutenberg, 2006), chap. XVII, part III, https://www.gutenberg.org/files/815/815-h/815-h.htm.
2. de Tocqueville, *Democracy in America*, chap. XVII, part II.
3. de Tocqueville, *Democracy in America*, chap. XVII, part II.
4. "The Mayflower Compact," Independence Hall Association, accessed June 15, 2020, https://www.ushistory.org/documents/mayflower.htm.
5. "Dr. Dobson's December Newsletter," Dr. James Dobson's Family Talk, accessed June 23, 2020, http://www.drjamesdobson.org/news/commentaries/archives/2017-newsletters/december-newsletter-2017.
6. Ed Stetzer, "Christianity Isn't Dying, *Cultural* Christianity Is," Crosswalk.com, October 23, 2012, https://www.crosswalk.com/church/pastors-or-leadership/christianity-isn-t-dying-i-cultural-i-christianity-is.html.
7. Stetzer, "Christianity Isn't Dying, *Cultural* Christianity Is."
8. Stetzer, "Christianity Isn't Dying, *Cultural* Christianity Is."
9. Stetzer, "Christianity Isn't Dying, *Cultural* Christianity Is."

10. Stetzer, "Christianity Isn't Dying, *Cultural* Christianity Is."

11. Stetzer, "Christianity Isn't Dying, *Cultural* Christianity Is."

12. Stetzer, "Christianity Isn't Dying, *Cultural* Christianity Is."

13. Revelation 19:7.

14. Ryan P. Burge, "Plenty of the 'Nones' Actually Head Back to Church," *Christianity Today*, February 6, 2018, https://www.christianitytoday.com/news/2018/february/ nones-agnostics-religious-identity-switching-cces-christian.html.

15. "America's Changing Religious Landscape," Pew Research Center, May 12, 2015, https://www.pewforum. org/2015/05/12/americas-changing-religious-landscape/.

16. Burge, "Plenty of the 'Nones' Actually Head Back to Church."

17. Burge, "Plenty of the 'Nones' Actually Head Back to Church."

18. Allan W. Eckert, *A Sorrow in Our Heart* (New York: Bantam Books, 1992), 673, https://www.amazon.com/ Sorrow-Our-Heart-Life-Tecumseh/dp/055356174X.

19. James B. Finley, *The Autobiography of James B. Finley; or Pioneer Life in the West*, ed. W. P. Strickland (Cincinnati: R. P. Thompson, 1853), 238, https://books.google.com/ books?id=HCIFAAAAYAAJ.

20. James B. McFerrin, *History of Methodism in Tennessee*, vol. 2 (Nashville: Southern Methodist Publishing House, 1871), 263, https://books.google.com/ books?id=99EQAAAAIAAJ.

21. Luke 21:26.

22. David R. Schilling, "Knowledge Doubling Every 12 Months, Soon to Be Every 12 Hours," Industry Tap, April 19, 2013, https://www.industrytap.com/knowledge-doubling-every-12-months-soon-to-be-every-12-hours/3950.

23. Stephen Mansfield, *Mansfield's Book of Manly Men: An Utterly Invigorating Guide to Being Your Most Masculine Self* (Nashville: Nelson Books, 2013), 140, https://books.google.com/books?id=HAJKgiJSRiMC.

24. Ephesians 4:2.

25. Melissa Locker, "Kids Raised Going to Church May Be Happier Adults, Study Says," *Southern Living*, November 8, 2018, https://www.msn.com/en-us/health/ pregnancyparenting/kids-raised-going-to-church-are- happier-adults-study-finds/ar-BBPsnGj.

26. Locker, "Kids Raised Going to Church May Be Happier Adults, Study Says."

27. Ying Chen and Tyler J. VanderWeele, "Associations of Religious Upbringing With Subsequent Health and Well-Being From Adolescence to Young Adulthood: An Outcome-Wide Analysis," *American Journal of Epidemiology* 187, no. 11 (2018): 2355–64, https://www. ncbi.nlm.nih.gov/pmc/articles/PMC6211237/.

28. Studylight.org, s.v. *"philóxenos,"* accessed June 16, 2020, https://www.studylight.org/lexicons/greek/5382.html.

29. Rick Richardson, *Reimagining Evangelism: Inviting Friends on a Spiritual Journey* (Downers Grove, IL: IVP Books, 2006), 50.

30. Jeff Christopherson, "The Power of Biblical Hospitality," *Christianity Today*, August 19, 2019, https://www. christianitytoday.com/edstetzer/2019/august/power-of- biblical-hospitality-entertainment-jesus.html.

31. Christopherson, "The Power of Biblical Hospitality."

32. C.S. Lewis, *Letters to Malcolm: Chiefly on Prayer* (1964; repr., New York: HarperOne, 2017), 2.

My FREE GIFT to You

Dear Reader,

I am so happy you read my book. This moment in American history is a reprieve. It is a moment to take stock. It is a moment to focus on the future. And it starts in you.

As a thank-you…
I am offering you a gift:

E-book: *Peace for Your Mind, Hope for Your Heart*

To get this **FREE GIFT**, please go to:

TimClintonBooks.com/freegift

Thanks again, and God bless you,

Dr. Tim Clinton